Frank Moore

Songs and Ballads of the Southern People. 1861-1865

Frank Moore

Songs and Ballads of the Southern People. 1861-1865

ISBN/EAN: 9783744766104

Printed in Europe, USA, Canada, Australia, Japan

Cover: Foto ©Thomas Meinert / pixelio.de

More available books at **www.hansebooks.com**

SONGS AND BALLADS

OF THE

SOUTHERN PEOPLE.

1861–1865.

COLLECTED AND EDITED

BY

FRANK MOORE.

NEW YORK:
D. APPLETON AND COMPANY,
1, 3, AND 5 BOND STREET.
1886.

COPYRIGHT, 1886,
BY D. APPLETON AND COMPANY.

All rights reserved.

NOTE TO READERS.

THIS collection has been made with the view of preserving in permanent form the opinions and sentiments of the Southern people, as embodied in their Songs and Ballads of 1861–1865; which, better than any other medium, exhibit the temper of the times and popular feeling. The historical value of the productions is admitted. Age will not impair it.

The editor has endeavored to give the best of the inspirations. A desire to announce the authorship of the pieces has been gratified in most instances. Where requests have been made not to give names and places and circumstances, by whom, and where they have been written, they have been regarded, the spirit, meaning and intent not being affected, nor in the least abated by such a course. To those who have assisted in collecting, the editor returns his thanks. After this volume reaches those who are interested, should any of them desire to correct mistakes that may have crept into it, he will be glad to make the changes required.

Should any one, into whose hands the volume may fall, know of copies of songs or ballads, or of letters and incidents upon which such are founded —songs and ballads, letters or incidents not already collected in book form—the editor will be glad to be advised, that means may be taken for their permanent preservation, which he is using every endeavor to secure. A postal card, giving name and residence, addressed to him, in the care of his publishers, D. Appleton and Company, New York City, will receive immediate attention.

The essence of history exists in its songs. Those that are carried in the memory are earliest forgotten. It is a praiseworthy plan that saves all. Will those who "know them by heart," and have "sung them in camp and in battle," help to rescue them from oblivion?

FRANK MOORE.

NEW YORK, *January*, 1886.

SONGS

OF THE

SOUTHERN PEOPLE.

A POEM FOR THE TIMES.

BY JOHN R. THOMPSON.

Who talks of Coercion? Who dares to deny
   A resolute people their right to be free?
Let him blot out forever one star from the sky,
   Or curb with his fetter one wave of the sea.

Who prates of Coercion? Can love be restored
   To bosoms where only resentment may dwell;
Can peace upon earth be proclaimed by the sword,
   Or good-will among men be established by shell?

Shame! shame that the statesman and trickster, forsooth,
   Should have for a crisis no other recourse,
Beneath the fair day-spring of Light and of Truth,
   Than the old *brutum fulmen* of Tyranny,—
   Force.

From the holes where Fraud, Falsehood, and Hate slink away;
From the crypt in which Error lies buried in chains;
This foul apparition stalks forth to the day,
   And would ravage the land which his presence profanes.

Could you conquer us, Men of the North, could you bring
   Desolation and death on our homes as a flood;
Can you hope the pure lily, Affection, will spring
   From ashes all reeking and sodden with blood?

Could you brand us as villeins and serfs, know ye not
   What fierce, sullen hatred lurks under the scar?
How loyal to Hapsburg is Venice, I wot;
   How dearly the Pole loves his Father, the Czar!

But 'twere well to remember this land of the sun
  Is a *nutrix leonum*, and suckles a race
Strong-armed, lion-hearted, and banded as one,
  Who brook not oppression and know not disgrace.

And well may the schemers in office beware
  The swift retribution that waits upon crime,
When the lion, RESISTANCE, shall leap from his lair,
  With a fury that renders his vengeance sublime.

Once, men of the North, we were brothers, and still,
  Though brothers no more, we would gladly be friends;
Nor join in a conflict accurst, that must fill
  With ruin the country on which it descends.

But if smitten with blindness, and mad with the rage
  The gods give to all whom they wished to destroy,
You would act a new Iliad to darken the age,
  With horrors beyond what is told us of Troy:

If, deaf as the adder itself to the cries,
  When Wisdom, Humanity, Justice implore,
You would have our proud eagle to feed on the eyes
  Of those who have taught him so grandly to soar:

If there be to your malice no limit imposed,
  And your reckless design is to rule with the rod
The men upon whom you have already closed
  Our goodly domain and the temples of God:

To the breeze then your banner dishonored unfold,
  And at once let the tocsin be sounded afar;
We greet you, as greeted the Swiss Charles the Bold,
  With a farewell to peace and a welcome to war!

For the courage that clings to our soil, ever bright,
  Shall catch inspiration from turf and from tide;
Our sons unappalled shall go forth to the fight,
  With the smile of the fair, the pure kiss of the bride;

And the bugle its echoes shall send through the past,
In the trenches of Yorktown to waken the slain;
While the sods of King's Mountain shall heave at the blast,
And give up its heroes to glory again.
Charleston Mercury.

ETHNOGENESIS.

BY HENRY TIMROD.*

I.

HATH not the morning dawned with added light?
And will not evening call another star
Out of the infinite regions of the night,
To mark this day in heaven? At last we are
A nation among nations; and the world
Shall soon behold in many a distant part
   Another flag unfurled!
Now, come what may, whose favor need we court?

---

* Written on the occasion of the meeting of the Confederate Congress, at Montgomery, February 4, 1861, and published in the "Charleston Courier."

And, under God, whose thunder need we
  fear?
  Thank him who placed us here
Beneath so kind a sky—the very sun
Takes part with us; and on our errands run
All breezes of the ocean; dew and rain
Do noiseless battle for us; and the year
And all the gentle daughters in her train
March in our ranks, and in our service wield
  Long spears of golden grain!
A yellow blossom as her fairy shield
June flings our azure banner to the wind,
  While in the order of their birth
Her sisters pass, and many an ample field
Grows white beneath their steps, till now behold
  Its endless sheets unfold
The snow of Southern summers! Let the
  earth
Rejoice! beneath those fleeces soft and warm
    Our happy land shall sleep
    In a repose as deep
    As if we lay intrenched behind
Whole leagues of Russian ice and Arctic
  storm!

II.

And what, if mad with wrongs themselves have wrought,
    In their own treachery caught,
    By their own fears made bold,
    And leagued with him of old,
Who long since in the limits of the North
Set up his evil throne, and warred with God—
What if, both mad and blinded in their rage,
Our foes should fling us down their mortal gage,
And with a hostile step profane our sod!
We shall not shrink, my brothers, but go forth
To meet them, marshaled by the Lord of Hosts,
And overshadowed by the mighty ghosts
Of Moultrie and of Eutaw—who shall foil
Auxiliars such as these? Nor these alone,
    But every stock and stone
Shall help us; but the very soil,
And all the generous wealth it gives to toil,
And all for which we love our noble land,
Shall fight beside, and through us, sea and strand,
    The heart of woman, and her hand,

Tree, fruit, and flower, and every influence
    Gentle or grave or grand.
    The winds in our defense
Shall seem to blow; to us the hills shall lend
  Their firmness and their calm;
And in our stiffened sinews we shall blend
  The strength of pine and palm!

III.

Look where we will, we can not find a ground
  For any mournful song:
Call up the clashing elements around,
  And test the right and wrong!
On one side, pledges broken, creeds that lie,
Religion sunk in vague philosophy,
Empty professions, pharisaic leaven,
Souls that would sell their birthright in the sky,
Philanthropists who pass the beggar by,
And laws which controvert the laws of Heaven.
And, on the other—first, a righteous cause!
  Then, honor without flaws,
Truth, Bible reverence, charitable wealth,
And for the poor and humble, laws which give,
Not the mean right to buy the right to live,

But life, and home, and health.
To doubt the issue were distrust in God!
If in his Providence he hath decreed
That to the peace for which we pray,
Through the Red Sea of War must lie our way,
Doubt not, O brothers, we shall find at need
   A Moses with his rod!

IV.

But let our fears—if fears we have—be still,
And turn us to the future! Could we climb
Some Alp in thought, and view the coming time,
We should indeed behold a sight to fill
   Our eyes with happy tears!
Not for the glories which a hundred years
Shall bring us; not for lands from sea to sea,
And wealth, and power, and peace, though these
   shall be;
But for the distant peoples we shall bless,
And the hushed murmurs of a world's distress:
For, to give food and clothing to the poor,
   The whole sad planet o'er,
And save from crime its humblest human door,
Our mission is! The hour is not yet ripe
When all shall see it, but behold the type

Of what we are and shall be to the world,
In our own grand and genial Gulf stream furled,
Which through the vast and colder ocean pours
Its waters, so that far-off Arctic shores
May sometimes catch upon the softened breeze
Strange tropic warmth and hints of summer seas.

THE SOUTHERN CROSS.

BY ST. GEORGE TUCKER.

Air—*The Star Spangled Banner.*

Oh, say, can you see, through the gloom and the storm,
  More bright for the darkness, that pure constellation?
Like the symbol of love and redemption its form,
  As it points to the haven of hope for the nation.
    How radiant, each star, as the beacon afar,
    Giving promise of peace, or assurance in war;

'Tis the Cross of the South, which shall
  ever remain,
To light us to Freedom and Glory again!

How peaceful and blest was America's soil,
  Till betrayed by the guile of the Puritan
    demon,
Which lurks under virtue, and springs from its
    coil
  To fasten its fangs in the life-blood of free-
    men.
    Then loudly appeal, to each heart that can
      feel,
    And crush the foul viper 'neath Liberty's
      heel!
    And the Cross of the South shall forever
      remain,
    To light us to Freedom and Glory again!

'Tis the emblem of peace, 'tis the day-star of
    hope,
  Like the sacred Labarum, which guided the
    Roman;
From the shores of the Gulf to the Delaware's
    slope,

'Tis the trust of the free, and the terror of foemen.
 Fling its folds to the air, while we boldly declare
 The rights we demand, or the deeds that we dare;
 And the Cross of the South shall forever remain,
 To light us to Freedom and Glory again!

But if peace should be hopeless, and justice denied,
 And war's bloody vulture should flap his black pinions,
Then gladly to arms! while we hurl in our pride,
 Defiance to tyrants, and death to their minions,
 With our front to the field, swearing never to yield,
 Or return, like the Spartan, in death on our shield;
 And the Cross of the South shall triumphantly wave
 As the flag of the Free, or the pall of the brave.

Southern Literary Messenger.

HARP OF THE SOUTH, AWAKE!

BY J. M. KILGOUR.

Harp of the South, awake!
    From every golden wire,
Let the voice of thy power go forth,
    Like the rush of a prairie fire;
With the rush and the rhythm of a power
    That dares a freeman's grave,
Rather than live to wear
    The chains of a truckling slave.

Harp of the South, awake!
    Thy sons are aroused at last,
And their legions are gathering now,
    To the sound of the trumpet blast;
To the scream of the piercing fife,
    And the beat of the rolling drum,
From mountain, and hill, and plain,
    And field, and town, they come.

Harp of the South, awake!
    Their banners are on the breeze;
Tell the world how vain the thought
    To subdue such men as these,

With hero hearts that beat,
  To the throbs of the spirit-flame,
Which will kindle their battle-fires
  In freedom's holy name.

Harp of the South, awake!
  But not to sing of love,
In shady forest-bower,
  Or fragrant orange grove;
Oh, no, but thy song must be
  The wrath of the battle crash,
Inscribed on the cloud of war,
  With the pen of its lightning flash.

Harp of the South, awake!
  And strike the strains once more,
Which nerved thy heroes' hearts
  In the glorious days of yore;
Which gave a giant's strength
  To the arm of MARION,
Of SUMTER, MORGAN, LEE,
  And your own great WASHINGTON.

Harp of the South, awake!
  Your freedom's angel calls,
In the laugh of the rippling rills,
  And the roar of the waterfalls.

See how she bends to hear,
  As she walks the valleys through,
And along the mountain tops,
  In robes of gold and blue.

Harp of the South, awake!
  The proud, the full-soul'd South—
With the dusk of her flashing eyes,
  And the lure of her rosy mouth—
With love, or pride, or wrath,
  Thrilling her noble form,
As she smiles like a summer sky,
  Or frowns like a summer storm!

Harp of the South, awake!
  Though the soldier's beaming tear
May fall on thy trembling strings,
  As he breathes his farewell prayer;
Yet, tell him how to die
  On the bloody battle-field,
Rather than to her foes
  The gallant South should yield.*

---

* These lines were published, and respectfully dedicated to Captain Bradley T. Johnson, of the Frederick (Md.) Volunteers, now (1861) in service in Virginia, by his friend J. M. Kilgour, their author.

ARISE.

BY C. G. POYNAS.

Carolinians! who inherit
   Blood which flowed in patriot veins!
Rouse ye from lethargic slumber,
   Rouse and fling away your chains!
From the mountain to the seaboard,
   Let the cry be—Up! Arise!
Throw our pure Palmetto banner
   Proudly upward to the skies.

Fling it out! its lone star beaming
   Brightly to the nation's gaze;
Lo! another star arises!
   Quickly, proudly *it* emblaze!
Yet another! Bid it welcome
   With a hearty "three times three";
Send it forth, on boom of cannon,
   Southern men will *dare be free*.

Faster than the cross of battle
   Summoned rude Clan Alpine's host,
Flash the news from sea to mountain—
   Back from mountain to the coast!

On the lightning's wing it fleeth,
   Scares the eagle in his flight,
As his keen eye sees arising
   Glory, yet shall daze his sight!

Cease the triumph—days of darkness
   Loom upon us from afar:
Can a woman's voice for battle
   Ring the fatal note of war?
Yes—when we have borne aggression
   Till submission is disgrace—
Southern women call for *action;*
   Ready would the danger face!

Yes, in many a matron's bosom
   Burns the Spartan spirit now;
From the maiden's eye it flashes,
   Glows upon her snowy brow;
E'en our infants in their prattle
   Urge us on to *risk our all*—
"Would we leave them, as a blessing.
   The oppressor's hateful thrall?"

No!—then up, true-hearted Southrons,
   Like bold "giants nerved by wine";
Never fear! The cause is holy—
   It is sacred—yea, divine!

For the Lord of Hosts is with us,
  It is *He* has cast our lot;
Blest our homes—from lordly mansion
  To the humblest negro cot.

God of battles! hear our cry—
  Give us nerve to *do* or *die!*

THE STAR OF THE WEST.

I wish I was in de land o' cotton,
Old times dair ain't not forgotten—
  Look away, etc.
In Dixie land whar I was born in,
Early on one frosty mornin'—
  Look away, etc.
    Chorus—Den I wish I was in Dixie.

In Dixie land dat frosty mornin',
Jis 'bout de time de day was dawnin',
  Look away, etc.
De signal fire from de east bin roarin',
Rouse up, Dixie, no more snorin'—
  Look away, etc.
      Den I wish I was in Dixie.

Dat rocket high a blazing in de sky,
'Tis de sign dat de snobbies am comin' up nigh—
    Look away, etc.
Dey bin braggin' long, if we dare to shoot a shot,
Dey comin' up strong and dey'll send us all to pot.
    Fire away, fire away, lads in gray.
           Den I wish I was in Dixie.
              Charleston Mercury.

FAREWELL TO BROTHER JONATHAN.

BY "CAROLINE."

FAREWELL! we must part; we have turned from the land
Of our cold-hearted brother, with tyrannous hand,
Who assumed all our rights as a favor to grant,
And whose smile ever covered the sting of a taunt;

Who breathed on the fame he was bound to defend—
Still the craftiest foe, 'neath the guise of a friend;

Who believed that our bosoms would bleed at
    a touch,
Yet could never believe he could goad them too
    much;

Whose conscience affects to be seared with our
    sin,
Yet is plastic to take all its benefits in;
The mote in our eye so enormous has grown,
That he never perceives there's a beam in his
    own.

O Jonathan, Jonathan! vassal of pelf,
Self-righteous, self-glorious, yes, every inch self,
Your loyalty now is all bluster and boast,
But was dumb when the foemen invaded our coast.

In vain did your country appeal to you then,
You coldly refused her your money and men;
Your trade interrupted, you slunk from her wars,
And preferred British gold to the Stripes and the
    Stars!

Then our generous blood was as water poured
    forth,
And the sons of the South were the shields of
    the North;

Nor our patriot ardor one moment gave o'er,
Till the foe you had fed we had driven from the shore!

Long years we have suffered opprobrium and wrong,
But we clung to your side with affection so strong,
That at last, in mere wanton aggression, you broke
All the ties of our hearts with one murderous stroke.

We are tired of contest for what is our own,
We are sick of a strife that could never be done;
Thus our love has died out, and its altars are dark,
Not Prometheus's self could rekindle the spark.

O Jonathan, Jonathan! deadly the sin
Of your tigerish thirst for the blood of your kin;
And shameful the spirit that gloats over wives
And maidens despoiled of their honor and lives!

Your palaces rise from the fruits of our toil,
Your millions are fed from the wealth of our soil;
The balm of our air brings the health to your cheek,
And our hearts are aglow with the welcome we speak.

O brother! beware how you seek us again,
Lest you brand on your forehead the signet of Cain;
That blood and that crime on your conscience must sit;
We may fall—we may perish—but never submit!

The pathway that leads to the Pharisee's door
We remember, indeed, but we tread it no more;
Preferring to turn, with the Publican's faith,
To the path through the valley and shadow of death!

THE UNIFORM OF GRAY.

BY EVAN ELBERT.

The Briton boasts his coat of red,
  With lace and spangles decked;
In garb of green the French are seen,
  With gaudy colors flecked;
The Yankees strut in dingy blue,
  And epaulets display;
Our Southern girls more proudly view
  The uniform of gray.

That dress is worn by gallant hearts
  Who every foe defy,
Who stalwart stand, with battle-brand,
  To conquer or to die!
They fight for freedom, hope and home,
  And honor's voice obey,
And proudly wear where'er they roam
  The uniform of gray.

What though 'tis stained with crimson hues,
  And dim with dust and smoke,
By bullets torn, and rent and shorn
  By many a hostile stroke;

The march, the camp, the bivouac,
   The onset and the fray
But only serve more dear to make
   The uniform of gray.

When wild war's tiger-strife is past,
   And liberty restored;
When independence reigns at last,
   By valor's arm secured;
The South will stand, erect and grand,
   And loftiest honors pay
To those who bore her flag, and wore
   The uniform of gray.

And woman's love, man's best reward,
   Shall cluster round their path,
And soothe and cheer the volunteer
   Who dared the foeman's wrath.
Bright wreaths she'll bring, and roses fling
   Around his triumph-way,
And long in song thy fame prolong
   Old uniform of gray.

"WE CONQUER OR DIE."

BY JAMES PIERPONT.

The war drum is beating, prepare for the fight,
The stern bigot Northman exults in his might,
Gird on your bright weapons, your foemen are nigh;
Let this be our watchword, "We conquer or die!"

The trumpet is sounding from mountain to shore,
Your swords and your lances must slumber no more,
Fling forth to the sunlight your banner on high,
Inscribed with the watchword, "We conquer or die!"

March to the battlefield, there do or dare,
With shoulder to shoulder, all danger to share,
And let your proud watchword ring up to the sky,
Till the blue arch re-echoes "We conquer or die!"

Press forward undaunted, nor think of retreat,
The enemy's host on the threshold to meet;
Strike firm till the foeman before you shall fly,
Appalled by the watchword, "We conquer or die!"

Go forth in the pathway our forefathers trod;
We, too, fight for freedom—our Captain is God;
Their blood in our veins, with their honor we vie,
Theirs, too, was the watchword, "We conquer or die!"

We strike for the South—mountain, valley and plain—
For the South we will conquer again and again;
Her day of salvation and triumph is nigh,
Ours, then, be the watchword, "We conquer or die!"

SONS OF FREEDOM.

BY NANNY GRAY.

Sons of freedom, on to glory
   Go, where brave men *do* or *die*,
Let your names in future story
   Gladden every patriot's eye;
'Tis your country calls you, hasten!
   Backward hurl the invading foe;
Freemen never think of danger,—
   To the glorious battle go!

Oh! remember gallant Jackson,
   Single-handed in the fight,
Death-blows dealt the fierce marauder,
   For his liberty and right;
Tho' he fell beneath their *thousands*,
   Who that covets not his fame?
Grand and glorious, brave and noble,
   Henceforth shall be Jackson's name.

Sons of freedom, can you linger
   When you hear the battle's roar,
Fondly dallying with your pleasures
   When the foe is at your door?
Never! no! we fear no idlers,
   "Death or freedom"'s now the cry,
'Till the *stars* and *bars*, triumphant,
   Spread their folds to every eye.
                    Richmond Whig.

"CALL ALL! CALL ALL!"

BY "GEORGIA."

WHOOP! the Doodles have broken loose,
Roaring round like the very deuce!

Lice of Egypt, a hungry pack,—
After 'em, boys, and drive 'em back.

Bull-dog, terrier, cur, and fice,
Back to the beggarly land of ice;
Worry 'em, bite 'em, scratch and tear
Everybody and everywhere.

Old Kentucky is caved from under,
Tennessee is split asunder,
Alabama awaits attack,
And Georgia bristles up her back.

Old John Brown is dead and gone!
Still his spirit is marching on,—
Lantern-jawed, and legs, my boys,
Long as an ape's from Illinois!

Want a weapon? Gather a brick,
Club or cudgel, or stone or stick;
Anything with a blade or butt,
Anything that can cleave or cut.

Anything heavy, or hard, or keen!
Any sort of slaying machine!
Anything with a willing mind,
And the steady arm of a man behind.

Want a weapon? Why, capture one!
Every Doodle has got a gun,
Belt, and bayonet, bright and new;
Kill a Doodle, and capture *two!*

Shoulder to shoulder, son and sire!
All, call all! to the feast of fire!
Mother and maiden, and child and slave,
A common triumph or a single grave.
Rockingham, Va., Register.

THE ORDERED AWAY.

Dedicated to the Oglethorpe and Walker Light Infantries.

BY MRS. J. J. JACOBUS.

At the end of each street, a banner we meet,
   The people all march in a mass,
But quickly aside, they step back with pride,
   To let the brave companies pass.
The streets are dense filled, but the laughter is still'd—
   The crowd is all going one way;
Their cheeks are blanched white, but they smile as they light
   Lift their hats to the—Ordered away.

They smile while the dart deeply pierces their
    heart,
  But each eye flashes back the war-glance,
As they watch the brave file march up with a
    smile,
  'Neath their flag—with their muskets and lance;
The cannon's loud roar vibrates on the shore,
  But the people are quiet to-day,
As, startled, they see how fearless and free
  March the companies—Ordered away.

Not a quiver or gleam of fear can be seen,
  Though they go to meet death in disguise;
For the hot air is filled with poison distilled
  'Neath the rays of fair Florida's skies.
Hark! the drum and fife awake to new life
  The soldiers who—"Can't get away;"
Who *wish*, as they wave their hats to the brave,
  That *they* were the—Ordered away.

As *our* parting grows near, let us quell back
    the tear,
  Let our smiles shine as bright as of yore;
Let us stand with the mass, salute as they pass,
  And weep when we see them no more.

Let no tear-drop or sigh dim the light of our
    eye,
  Or move from our lips, as they say—
While waving our hand to a brave little band—
  Good-by to the—Ordered away.

Let them go, in God's name, in defense of their
    fame,
  Brave death at the cannon's wide mouth;
Let them honor and save the land of the
    brave,
  Plant Freedom's bright flag in the *South*.
Let them go! While we weep, and lone vigils
    keep,
  We will bless them, and fervently pray
To the God whom we trust, for our cause firm
    but just,
  And our loved ones—the Ordered away.

When fierce battles storm, we will rise up each
    morn,
  Teach our young sons the saber to wield:
Should their brave fathers die, we will arm *them* to
    fly
  And fill up the gap in the field.

Then, fathers and brothers, fond husbands and
    lovers,
  March! march bravely on! *We* will stay,
Alone in our sorrow, to pray on each morrow
  For our loved ones—the Ordered away.
    AUGUSTA, GA., *April* 2, 1861.

THE MARTYR OF ALEXANDRIA.

BY JAMES W. SIMMONS.

REVEALED, as in a lightning flash,
    A Hero stood!
The invading foe, the trumpet's crash,
    Set up his blood!

High o'er the sacred pile that bends
    Those forms above,
Thy Star, O Freedom! brightly blends
    Its rays with Love.

The banner of a mighty race
    Serenely there
Unfurls—the genius of the place,
    And haunted air!

A vow is registered in heaven—
    Patriot! 'twas thine
To guard those matchless colors, given
    By hand divine.

Jackson! thy spirit may not hear
    The wail ascend!
A nation bends above thy bier,
    And mourns its friend.

Thy example is thy monument;
    In organ tones
Thy name resounds, with glory blent,
    Prouder than thrones!

And they whose loss has been our gain—
    A People's care
Shall win their hearts from pain,
    And wipe the tear.

When time shall set the captive free,
    Now scathed by wrath,
Heirs of his immortality,
    Bright be their path.

INDIANOLA, TEXAS.

DIXIE.

Southrons, hear your Country call you!

BY ALBERT PIKE.

SOUTHRONS, hear your Country call you!
Up! lest worse than death befall you!
  To arms! To arms! To arms! in Dixie!
Lo! all the beacon-fires are lighted,
Let all hearts be now united!

    To arms! To arms! To arms! in Dixie!
      Advance the flag of Dixie!
          Hurrah! hurrah!
    For Dixie's land we take our stand,
      And live or die for Dixie!
      To arms! To arms!
        And conquer peace for Dixie!
      To arms! To arms!
        And conquer peace for Dixie!

Hear the Northern thunders mutter!
Northern flags in South wind flutter;
    To arms, etc.,
        Advance the flag of Dixie! etc.

Fear no danger! Shun no labor!
Lift up rifle, pike, and saber!
  To arms, etc.
Shoulder pressing close to shoulder,
Let the odds make each heart bolder!
  To arms, etc.
    Advance the flag of Dixie! etc.

How the South's great heart rejoices,
At your cannons' ringing voices;
  To arms! etc.
For faith betrayed and pledges broken,
Wrongs inflicted, insults spoken;
  To arms! etc.
    Advance the flag of Dixie! etc.

Strong as lions, swift as eagles,
Back to their kennels hunt these beagles;
  To arms! etc.
Cut the unequal words asunder!
Let them then each other plunder!
  To arms! etc.
    Advance the flag of Dixie! etc.

Swear upon your country's altar,
Never to submit or falter!
  To arms! etc.

Till the spoilers are defeated,
Till the Lord's work is completed.
    To arms! etc.
        Advance the flag of Dixie! etc.

Halt not till our Federation
Secures among Earth's Powers its station!
    To arms! etc.
Then at peace, and crowned with glory,
Hear your children tell the story!
    To arms! etc.
        Advance the flag of Dixie! etc.

If the loved ones weep in sadness,
Victory soon shall bring them gladness:
    To arms! etc.
Exultant pride soon banish sorrow;
Smiles chase tears away to-morrow.
    To arms! etc.
        Advance the flag of Dixie! etc.

THE RIGHT ABOVE THE WRONG.

BY JOHN W. OVERALL.

In other days our fathers' love was loyal, full, and free,
For those they left behind them in the Island of the Sea;
They fought the battles of King George, and toasted him in song,
For them the Right kept proudly down the tyranny of Wrong.

But when the King's weak, willing slaves laid tax upon the tea,
The Western men rose up and braved the Island of the Sea;
And swore a fearful oath to God, those men of iron might,
That in the end the Wrong should die, and up should go the Right.

The King sent over hireling hosts—Briton, Hessian, Scot—
And swore in turn those Western men, when captured, should be shot;

While Chatham spoke with earnest tongue against
    the hireling throng,
And mournfully saw the Right go down, and
    place give to the Wrong.

But God was on the righteous side, and Gideon's
    sword was out,
With clash of steel, and rattling.drum, and free-
    man's thunder-shout;
And crimson torrents drenched the land through
    that long, stormy fight,
But in the end, hurrah! the Wrong was beaten
    by the Right!

And when again the foemen came from out the
    Northern Sea,
To desolate our smiling land and subjugate the
    free,
Our fathers rushed to drive them back, with
    rifles keen and long,
And swore a mighty oath, the Right should subju-
    gate the Wrong.

And while the world was looking on, the strife
    uncertain grew,
But soon aloft rose up our stars amid a field of blue;

For Jackson fought on red Chalmette, and won the glorious fight,
And then the Wrong went down, hurrah! and triumph crowned the Right!

The day has come again, when men who love the beauteous South,
To speak, if needs be, for the Right, though by the cannon's mouth;
For foes accursed of God and man, with lying speech and song,
Would bind, imprison, hang the Right, and deify the Wrong.

But canting knave of pen and sword, nor sanctimonious fool,
Shall ever win this Southern land, to cripple, bind, and rule;
We'll muster on each bloody plain, thick as the stars of night,
And, through the help of God, the Wrong shall perish by the Right.

New Orleans True Delta.

TO MY SOLDIER BROTHER.

BY SALLIE E. BALLARD.

WHEN softly gathering shades of ev'n
   Creep o'er the prairies broad and green,
And countless stars bespangle heav'n,
   And fringe the clouds with silv'ry sheen,
My fondest sigh to thee is giv'n,
My lonely wand'ring soldier-boy;
     And thoughts of thee
     Steal over me
Like ev'ning shades, my soldier boy.

My brother, though thou'rt far away,
   And dangers hurtle round thy path,
And battle lightnings o'er thee play,
   And thunders peal in awful wrath,
Think, whilst thou'rt in the hot affray,
Thy sister prays for thee, my boy.
     If fondest prayer
     Can shield thee there,
Sweet angels guard my soldier boy.

Thy proud young heart is beating high
   To clash of arms and cannons' roar;

That firm set lip and flashing eye
  Tell how thy heart is brimming o'er.
Be free and live, be free or die!
Be that thy motto now, my boy;
    And though thy name's
    Unknown to fame's
'Tis graven on my heart, my boy.

THE SOUTH IN ARMS.

BY REV. J. H. MARTIN.

OH! see ye not the sight sublime,
Unequaled in all previous time,
Presented in this Southern clime,
        The home of chivalry?

A warlike race of freemen stand,
With martial front and sword in hand,
Defenders of their native land,—
        The sons of Liberty.

Unawed by numbers, they defy
The tyrant North, nor will they fly,
Resolved to conquer or to die,
        And win a glorious name.

Sprung from renowned heroic sires,
Inflamed with patriotic fires,
Their bosoms burn with fierce desires,
      They thirst for victory.

'Tis not the love of bloody strife,
The horrid sacrifice of life,
But thoughts of mother, sister, wife,
      That stir their manly hearts.

A sense of honor bids them go,
To meet a hireling, ruthless foe,
And deal in wrath the deadly blow
      Which vengeance loud demands.

In freedom's sacred cause they fight,
For Independence, Justice, Right,
And to resist a desperate might.
And by Manassas' glorious name,
And by Missouri's fields of fame,
We hear them swear, with one acclaim,
      We'll triumph or we'll die!

MELT THE BELLS.

BY F. Y. ROCKETT.

MELT the bells, melt the bells,
Still the tinkling on the plain,
And transmute the evening chimes
Into war's resounding rhymes,
That the invaders may be slain
  By the bells.

Melt the bells, melt the bells,
That for years have called to prayer,
And, instead, the cannon's roar
Shall resound the valleys o'er,
That the foe may catch despair
  From the bells.

Melt the bells, melt the bells,
Though it cost a tear to part
With the music they have made,
Where the friends we love are laid,
With pale cheek and silent heart,
  'Neath the bells.

Melt the bells, melt the bells,
Into cannon, vast and grim,
And the foe shall feel the ire
From the heaving lungs of fire,
And we'll put our trust in Him,
    And the bells.

Melt the bells, melt the bells,
And when foes no more attack,
And the lightning cloud of war
Shall roll thunderless and far,
We will melt the cannon back
    Into bells.

Melt the bells, melt the bells,
And they'll peal a sweeter chime,
And remind of all the brave
Who have sunk to glory's grave,
And will sleep through coming time
    'Neath the bells.*

---

* These lines were written when General Beauregard appealed to the people of the South to contribute their bells, that they might be melted into cannon.

TO THE TORIES OF VIRGINIA.

"I speak this unto your shame."

In the ages gone by, when Virginia arose
  Her honor and truth to maintain,
Her sons round her banner would rally with pride,
  Determined to save it from stain.

No heart in those days was so false or so cold,
  That it did not exquisitely thrill
With a love and devotion that none would withhold,
  Until death the proud bosom should chill.

Was Virginia in danger? Fast, fast at her call,
  From the mountains e'en unto the sea,
Came up her brave children their mother to shield,
  And to die that she still might be free.

And a coward was he, who, when danger's dark cloud
  Overshadowed Virginia's fair sky,
Turned a deaf, careless ear, when her summons was heard,
  Or refused for her honor to die.

Oh! proud are the mem'ries of days that are past,
  And richly the heart thrills whene'er
We think of the brave who, their mother to save,
  Have died, as they lived, without fear.

But *now*, can it be that Virginia's name
  Fails to waken the homage and love
Of e'en one of her sons? Oh! cold, cold must be
  The heart that her name will not move.

When she rallies for freedom, for justice, and right,
  Will her sons, with a withering sneer,
Revile her, and taunt her with treason and shame,
  Or say she is moved by foul fear?

Will they tell her her glories have fled or grown pale?
  That she bends to a tyrant in shame?
Will they trample her glorious flag in the dust,
  Or load with reproaches her name?

Will they fly from her shores, or desert her in
    need?
Will *Virginians* their backs ever turn
On their mother, and fly when the danger is nigh,
    And her claim to their fealty spurn?

False, false is the heart that refuses to yield
    The love that Virginia doth claim;
And base is the tongue that could utter the lie,
    That charges his mother with shame.

A blot on her 'scutcheon! a stain on her name!
    Our heart's blood should wipe it away;
We should die for her honor, and count it a boon
    Her mandates to heed and obey.

But never, oh, never, let human tongue say
    She is false to her honor or fame!
She is true to her past—to her future she's true—
    And Virginia has never known shame.

Then shame on the dastard, the recreant fool,
    That *would strike, in the dark,* at her now;
That would coldly refuse her fair fame to uphold,
    That would basely prove false to his vow.

But no! it can not—it can never be true,
  That Virginia claims one single child,
That would ever prove false to his home or his
    God,
  Or be with foul treason defiled.

And the man that could succor her enemies *now*,
  Even though on her soil he were born,
Is so base, so inhuman, so false and so vile,
  That Virginia disowns him with scorn!
Richmond Examiner.

WAR SONG.

BY A. B. MEEK, OF MOBILE.

WOULDST thou have me love thee, dearest,
  With a woman's proudest heart,
Which shall ever hold thee nearest,
  Shrined in its inmost heart?
Listen, then! My country's calling
  On her sons to meet the foe!
Leave these groves of rose and myrtle,
  Drop the dreamy hand of love!
Like young Körner, scorn the turtle
  When the eagle screams above!

Dost thou pause? Let dotards dally—
   Do thou for thy country fight!
'Neath her noble emblem rally—
   "God! our country, and her right!"
Listen! now her trumpet's calling
   On her sons to meet the foe!
Woman's heart is soft and tender,
   But 'tis proud and faithful, too;
Shall she be her land's defender?
   Lover! soldier? up and do!

Seize thy father's ancient falchion,
   Which once flashed as freedom's star!
Till sweet peace—the bow and halcyon,
   Still'd the stormy strife of war!
Listen! now thy country's calling
   On her sons to meet the foe!
Sweet is love in moonlight bowers!
   Sweet the altar and the flame!
Sweet is spring-time with her flowers!
   Sweeter far the patriot's name!

Should the God who rules above thee
   Doom thee to a soldier's grave,
Hearts will break, but fame will love thee,
   Canonized among the brave!

Listen, then, thy country's calling
  On her sons to meet the foe!
Rather would I view thee lying
  On the last red field of life,
'Mid thy country's heroes dying,
  Than to be a dastard's wife.

SUMTER; A BALLAD OF 1861.

BY E. O. MURDEN.

'Twas on the twelfth of April,
  Before the break of day,
We heard the guns of Moultrie
  Give signal for the fray.

Anon across the waters
  There boomed the answering gun,
From North and South came flash on flash—
  The battle had begun.

The mortars belched their deadly food,
  And spiteful whizzed the balls,
A fearful storm of iron hailed
  On Sumter's doomèd walls.

SUMTER; A BALLAD OF 1861.

We watched the meteor flight of shell,
   And saw the lightning flash;
Saw where each fiery missile fell,
   And heard the sullen crash.

The morn was dark and cloudy,
   Yet, till the sun arose,
No answer to our gallant boys
   Came booming from our foes.

Then through the dark and murky clouds
   The morning sunlight came,
And forth from Sumter's frowning walls
   Burst sudden sheets of flame.

The shot and shell flew thick and fast,
   The war-dogs howling spoke,
And thundering came their angry roar,
   Through wreathing clouds of smoke.

Again to fight for liberty,
   Our gallant sons had come,
They smiled when came the bugle call,
   And laughed when tapped the drum.

From cotton- and from corn-field,
   From desk and forum too,
From work-bench and from anvil, came
   Our gallant boys and true.

A hireling band had come to awe,
   Our chains to rivet fast;
Yon lofty pile scowls on our homes,
   Seaward the hostile mast.

But gallant freemen man our guns—
   No mercenary host,
Who barter for their honor's price,
   And of their baseness boast.

Now came our stately matrons,
   And maidens too by scores;
Oh! Carolina's beauty shone
   Like love-lights on her shores.

See yonder, anxious gazing,
   Alone a matron stands,
The tear-drop glistening on each lid,
   And tightly clasped her hands.

For there, exposed to deadly fire,
   Her husband and her son—
"Father," she spake, and heavenward looked,
   "Father, thy will be done."

See yonder group of maidens,
   No joyous laughter now,
For cares lie heavy on each heart
   And cloud each anxious brow:

For brothers dear, and lovers fond,
   Are there amid the strife;
Tearful the sister's anxious gaze—
   Pallid the promised wife.

Yet breathed no heart one thought of fear,
   Prompt at their country's call,
They yielded forth their dearest hopes,
   And gave to honor all!

Now comes a message from below—
   Oh quick the tidings tell—
"At Moultrie and Fort Johnson, too,
   And Morris, all are well!"

Then mark the joyous brightening;
  See how each bosom swells;
That friends and loved ones all are safe,
  Each to the other tells.

All day the shot flew thick and fast,
  All night the cannon roared,
While wreathed in smoke stern Sumter stood,
  And vengeful answer poured.

Again the sun rose, bright and clear,
  'Twas on the thirteenth day,
While, lo! at prudent distance moored
  Five hostile vessels lay.

With choicest abolition crews—
  The bravest of *their* brave—
They'd come to pull our Crescent down
  And dig Secession's grave.

See, see, how Sumter's banner trails,
  They're signaling for aid,
See you no boats of armed men?
  Is yet no movement made?

Now densest smoke and lurid flames
    Burst out o'er Sumter's walls;
"The fort's on fire," 's the cry;
    Again for aid he calls.

See you no boats or vessels yet?
    Dare they not risk *one* shot,
To make report grandiloquent
    Of aid they rendered not?

Nor boat nor vessel leaves the fleet—
    "Let the old Major burn"—
We'll boast of that we would have done,
    If but—on our return.

Go back, go back ye cravens,
    Go back the way ye came;
Ye gallant, *would be*, men-of-war,
    Go! to your country's shame.

'Mid fiery storm of shot and shell,
    'Mid smoke and roaring flame,
See how Kentucky's gallant son
    Does honor to her name!

See how he answers gun for gun—
   Hurrah ! his flag is down !
The white ! the white ! Oh see it wave !
   Is echoed all around.

Now ring the bells a joyous peal,
   And rend with shouts the air,
We've torn the hated banner down,
   And placed the Crescent there.

All honor to our gallant boys,
   Bring forth the roll of fame,
And there in glowing lines inscribe
   Each patriot hero's name.

Spread, spread the tidings far and wide,
   Ye winds take up the cry :
"Our soil's redeemed from hateful yoke,
   We'll keep it pure or die."

REBELS.

Rebels! 'tis a holy name!
   The name our fathers bore,
When battling in the cause of Right,
Against the tyrant in his might,
   In the dark days of yore.

Rebels! 'tis our family name!
   Our father, Washington,
Was the arch-rebel in the fight,
And gave the name to us—a right
   Of father unto son.

Rebels! 'tis our given name!
   Our mother, Liberty,
Received the title with her fame,
In days of grief, of fear, and shame,
   When at her breast were we.

Rebels! 'tis our sealèd name!
   A baptism of blood!
The war—aye, and the din of strife—
The fearful contest, life for life—
   The mingled crimson flood.

Rebels! 'tis a patriot's name!
  In struggles it was given;
We bore it then when tyrants raved,
And through their curses 'twas engraved
  On the doomsday-book of heaven.

Rebels! 'tis our fighting name!
  For peace rules o'er the land,
Until they speak of craven woe—
Until our rights receive a blow,
  From foe's or brother's hand.

Rebels! 'tis our dying name!
  For, although life is dear,
Yet, freemen born and freemen bred,
We'd rather live as freemen dead,
  Than live in slavish fear.

Then call us rebels, if you will—
  We glory in the name;
For bending under unjust laws,
And swearing faith to an unjust cause,
  We count a greater shame.

Atlanta Confederacy.

THE HEART OF LOUISIANA.

BY HARRIET STANTON.

Oh! let me weep, while o'er our land
  Vile discord strides, with sullen brow,
And drags to earth, with ruthless hand,
  The flag no tyrant's power could bow!

Trailed in the dust, inglorious laid,
  While one by one her stars retire,
And pride and power pursue the raid,
  That bids our liberty expire.

Aye, let me weep! for surely Heaven
  In anger views the unholy strife;
And angels weep that thus is riven
  The tie that gave to Freedom life.

I can not shout—I will not sing
  Loud pæans o'er a severed tie;
And, draped in woe, in tears I fling
  Our State's new flag to greet the sky.

I can but choose, while senseless zeal
  And lawless hate are clothed with power,
The bitter cup; but still I feel
  The sadness of this parting hour!

I know that thousand hearts will bleed
  While loud huzzas the welkin rend;
The thoughtless crowd will shout, Secede!
  But ah! will this the conflict end?

Oh! let me weep and prostrate lie
  Low at the footstool of my God;
I can not breathe one note of joy,
  While yet I feel His chastening rod.

Sure, we have as a nation sinned—
  Let every heart its folly own,
And sackcloth, as a girdle, bind,
  And mourn our glorious Union gone!

Sisters, farewell! You know not half
  The pain your pride, injustice, give;
You spurn our cause, and lightly laugh,
  And hope no more the wrong shall live.
New Orleans Delta.

SOUTHERN SONG OF FREEDOM.

AIR—"*The Minstrel's Return.*"

A NATION has sprung into life
   Beneath the bright Cross of the South;
And now a loud call to the strife
   Rings out from the shrill bugle's mouth.
They gather from morass and mountain,
   They gather from prairie and mart,
To drink, at young Liberty's fountain,
   The nectar that kindles the heart.
      Then, hail to the land of the pine!
        The home of the noble and free;
      A palmetto wreath we'll entwine
        Round the altar of young Liberty!

Our flag, with its cluster of stars,
   Firm fixed in a field of pure blue,
All shining through red and white bars,
   Now gallantly flutters in view.
The stalwart and brave round it rally,
   They press to their lips every fold,
While the hymn swells from hill and from valley,
   "Be, God, with our Volunteers bold."
      Then, hail to the land of the pine! etc.

The invaders rush down from the North,
  Our borders are black with their hordes;
Like wolves for their victims they flock,
  While whetting their knives and their swords.
Their watchword is "Booty and Beauty,"
  Their aim is to steal as they go;
But Southrons act up to your duty,
  And lay the foul miscreants low.
    Then, hail to the land of the pine! etc.

The God of our fathers looks down
  And blesses the cause of the just;
His smile will the patriot crown
  Who tramples his chains in the dust.
March, march Southrons! shoulder to shoulder,
  One heart-throb, one shout for the cause;
Remember—the world's a beholder,
  And your bayonets are fixed at your doors!
    Then, hail to the land of the pine!
      The home of the noble and free;
    A palmetto wreath we'll entwine
      Round the altar of young Liberty.
J. H. H.

THERE'S NOTHING GOING WRONG.

Dedicated to " Old Abe."

There's a general alarm,
The South's begun to arm,
And every hill and glen
Pours forth its warrior men;
Yet, "There's nothing going wrong,"
Is the burden of my song.

Six States already out,
Beckon others on the route;
And the cry is "Still they come!"
From the Southern sunny home;
Yet, "There's nothing going wrong,"
Is the burden of my song.

There's a wail in the land,
From a want-stricken band;
And "Food! Food!" is the cry:
"Give us work or we die!"
Yet, "There's nothing going wrong,"
Is the burden of my song.

The sturdy farmer doth complain
Of low prices for his grain;

And the miller, with his flour,
Murmurs the dullness of the hour.
Yet, "There's nothing going wrong,"
Is the burden of my song.

The burly butcher in the mart,
He, too, also takes his part;
And the merchant in his store
Hears no creaking of his door.
But, "There's nothing going wrong,"
Is the burden of my song.

Stagnation is everywhere;
On the water, in the air,
In the shop, in the forge,
On the mount, in the gorge;
With the anvil, with the loom,
In the store and counting-room;
In the city, in the town,
With Mr. Smith, with Mr. Brown!
And "yet there's nothing wrong,
Is the burden of my song.

A. M. W.

NEW ORLEANS, *March* 4, 1861.

MARYLAND.

BY JAMES R. RANDALL.

The despot's heel is on thy shore,
    Maryland!
His torch is at thy temple door,
    Maryland!
Avenge the patriotic gore
That flecked the streets of Baltimore,
And be the battle-queen of yore,
    Maryland! My Maryland!

Hark to thy wand'ring son's appeal,
    Maryland!
My mother State! to thee I kneel,
    Maryland!
For life and death, for woe and weal,
Thy peerless chivalry reveal,
And gird thy beauteous limbs with steel,
    Maryland! My Maryland!

Thou wilt not cower in the dust,
    Maryland!
Thy beaming sword shall never rust,
    Maryland!

Remember Carroll's sacred trust;
Remember Howard's warlike thrust,—
And all thy slumberers with the just,
   Maryland! My Maryland!

Come! 'tis the red dawn of the day,
   Maryland!
Come! with thy panoplied array,
   Maryland!
With Ringgold's spirit for the fray,
With Watson's blood, at Monterey,
With fearless Lowe, and dashing May,
   Maryland! My Maryland!

Come! for thy shield is bright and strong,
   Maryland!
Come! for thy dalliance does thee wrong,
   Maryland!
Come! to thine own heroic throng,
That stalks with Liberty along,
And give a new *Key* to thy song,
   Maryland! My Maryland!

Dear Mother! burst the tyrant's chain,
   Maryland!
Virginia should not call in vain,
   Maryland!

She meets her sisters on the plain :
"*Sic semper*," 'tis the proud refrain,
That baffles minions back amain,
    Maryland !
Arise, in majesty again,
    Maryland ! My Maryland !

I see the blush upon thy cheek,
    Maryland !
But thou wast ever bravely meek,
    Maryland !
But lo ! there surges forth a shriek
From hill to hill, from creek to creek—
Potomac calls to Chesapeake,
    Maryland ! My Maryland !

Thou wilt not yield the Vandal toll,
    Maryland !
Thou wilt not crook to his control,
    Maryland !
Better the fire upon thee roll,
Better the blade, the shot, the bowl,
Than crucifixion of the soul,
    Maryland ! My Maryland !

I hear the distant thunder hum,
    Maryland!
The Old Line's bugle, fife and drum,
    Maryland!
She is not dead, nor deaf, nor dumb:
Huzza! she spurns the Northern scum!
She breathes—she burns! she'll come! she'll come!
    Maryland! My Maryland!

POINTE COUPEE, *April* 26, 1861.

A CRY TO ARMS.

BY HENRY TIMROD.

Ho! woodsmen of the mountain side!
    Ho! dwellers in the vales!
Ho! ye who by the chafing tide
    Have roughened in the gales!
Leave barn and byre, leave kin and cot,
    Lay by the bloodless spade;
Let desk, and case, and counter rot,
    And burn your books of trade!

A CRY TO ARMS.

The despot roves your fairest lands;
   And, till he flies or fears,
Your fields must grow but armèd hands,
   Your sheaves be sheaves of spears!
Give up to mildew and to rust
   The useless tools of gain,
And feed your country's sacred dust
   With floods of crimson rain!

Come, with the weapons at your call—
   With musket, pike, or knife:
He wields the deadliest blade of all
   Who lightest holds his life.
The arm that drives its unbought blows,
   With all a patriot's scorn,
Might brain a tyrant with a rose,
   Or stab him with a thorn!

Does any falter? Let him turn
   To some brave maiden's eyes,
And catch the holy fires that burn
   In those sublunar skies.
Oh! could you like your women feel,
   And in their spirit march,
A day might see your lines of steel
   Beneath the victor's arch.

What hope, O God! would not grow warm,
    When thoughts like these give cheer?
The Lily calmly braves the storm,
    And shall the Palm-tree fear?
No! rather let its branches court
    The rack that sweeps the plain,
And from the Lily's regal port
    Learn how to breast the strain!

Ho! woodsmen of the mountain side!
    Ho! dwellers in the vales!
Ho! ye who by the roaring tide
    Have roughened in the gales!
Come! flocking gayly to the fight,
    From forest, hill, and lake;
We battle for our Country's right,
    And for the Lily's sake!

NEW ORLEANS, *March* 9, 1862.

WAR SONG.*

Air—"*March, march, Ettrick and Teviotdale.*"

March, march on, brave "Palmetto" boys,
  "Sumter" and "Lafayettes" forward in order;
March, march, "Calhoun" and "Rifle" boys,
  All the base Yankees are crossing the *border*.
    Banners are round ye spread,
    Floating above your head,
Soon shall the *Lone Star* be famous in story,
    On, on, my gallant men,
    Vict'ry be thine again;
Fight for your *rights*, till the green sod is gory.
                  March, march, etc.

Young wives and sisters have buckled your armor on;
Maidens ye love bid ye *go* to the battle-field;
Strong arms and stout hearts have many a vict'ry won,
  Courage shall strengthen the weapons ye wield.

---

* The writer has a husband, three sons, two nephews, other relatives and friends, in the companies mentioned, to whom these lines are most respectfully inscribed.—*Charleston Mercury.*

Wild passions are storming,
Dark schemes are forming,
Deep snares are laid, but they *shall not* enthrall ye;
Justice your cause shall greet,
Laurels lay at your feet,
If each brave band be watchful and wary.
      March, march, etc.

Let fear and unmanliness vanish before ye;
Trust in the Rock who will shelter the righteous;
Plant *firmly* each step on the soil of the *free*—
A heritage left by the sires who bled for us.
May each heart be bounding,
When trumpets are sounding,
And the dark traitors shall strive to surround ye;
The great God of Battle
Can *still* the war-rattle,
And brighten the land with a sunset of glory.
      March, march, etc.

VIRGINIA—LATE BUT SURE!

BY W. H. HOLCOMBE.

The foe has hemmed us round: we stand at bay,
Here we will perish, or be free to-day!
  To drum and bugle sternly sounding,
  The Southern soldier's heart is bounding;
But stay—oh stay! Virginia is not here!
  Hush your strains of martial cheer;
    O bugle, peace!
    O war-drum, cease!
  Virginia is not here!
Suspend, O chief, your word of fight!
She will be soon in sight!
  Her children never called in vain!
    She comes not—comes not: the disgrace
  Were bitterer than the tyrant's chain!
    Oh, death! we dare thee face to face!

A gun! the foe's defiant shot—be still!
Hurrah! an answering gun behind the hill;
  And o'er its summit wildly streaming
  The squadrons of Virginia gleaming!*

---

* Virginia adopted her act of Secession on April 17, 1861.

Hurrah! hurrah! the Old Dominion comes!
  Blow your bugles! beat your drums!
    O doubt accurst!
    The last is first—
  The Old Dominion comes!
She grasps her thunderbolts of war;
Hurrah! hurrah! hurrah!
    Now loose, O chief! your battle storm!
    We hang impatient on your breath;
    Here in the flashing front we form!
    Virginia!—victory or death!

SOUTHERN SENTIMENT.

BY REV. A. M. BOX.

THE North may think that the South will yield,
  And seek for a place in the Union again;
But never will Southrons abandon the field
  And place themselves under *tyrannical reign*.

Sooner by far would we yield to the grave,
  Than form an alliance with so hated a foe;
To join the "old Union" would be to enslave
  Ourselves, our children, in want and in woe!

What! sons of the South! submit to be ruled
  By the minions of Abraham Lincoln, the fool?
Our fair ones insulted—our wealth all controlled
  By Yankees, free negroes, and every such tool!

Heaven forbid it! and arm us with might,
  To drive back our foes, and grind them to dust!
In every conflict may we put them to flight,
  Aided by thee, thou God of the just!

Our bosoms we'll bare to the glorious strife,
  And our oath is recorded on high,
To prevail in the cause is dearer than life,
  Or crushed in its ruins to die!

The battle is not to the strong we know,
  But to the just, the true, and the brave—
With faith in our GOD, right onward we'll go,
  Our country, our loved ones, to save.

THE SOUTHRON'S WAR-SONG.

BY J. A. WAGENER.

Arise! arise! with main and might,
    Sons of the sunny clime!
Gird on the sword; the sacred fight
    The holy hour doth chime.
Arise! the craven host draws nigh,
    In thundering array;
Arise, ye brave! let cowards fly—
    The hero bides the fray.

Strike hard, strike hard, thou noble band;
    Strike hard, with arm of fire!
Strike hard, for God and fatherland,
    For mother, wife, and sire!
Let thunders roar, the lightning flash;
    Bold Southron, never fear!
The bayonet's point, the saber's clash,
    True Southrons do and dare!

Bright flow'rs spring from the hero's grave;
    The craven knows no rest!
Thrice curs'd the traitor and the knave!
    The hero thrice is bless'd.

Then let each noble Southron stand,
  With bold and manly eye:
We'll do for God and fatherland;
  We'll do, we'll do, or die!

Charleston Courier.

JUSTICE IS OUR PANOPLY.

BY DE G.

WE'RE free from Yankee despots,
  We've left the foul mud-sills,
Declared for e'er our freedom—
  We'll keep it spite of ills.

Bring forth your scum and rowdies,
  Thieves, vagabonds, and all;
March down your Seventh Regiment,
  Battalions great and small.

We'll meet you in Virginia,
  A Southern battle-field,
Where Southern men will never
  To Yankee foemen yield.

Equip your Lincoln cavalry,
  Your NEGRO *light*-brigade,
Your hodmen, bootblacks, tinkers,
  And scum of every grade.

Pretended love for negroes
  Incites you to the strife;
Well, come each Yankee white man,
  And take a negro wife.

You'd make fit black companions,
  Black heart joined to black skin;
Such *unions* would be glorious—
  They'd make the Devil grin.

Our freedom is our panoply—
  Come on, you base *black*-guards,
We'll snuff you like wax-candles,
  Led by our Beauregards.

P. G. T. B. is not alone,
  Men like him with him fight;
God's providence is o'er us,
  He will protect the right.

THE BLUE COCKADE.

BY MARY WALSINGHAM CREAN.

God be with the laddie, who wears the blue cockade!
  He's gone to fight the battles of our darling Southern land;
He was true to old Columbia, till more sacred ties forbade—
  Till 'twere treason to obey her, when he took his sword in hand;
And God be with the laddie, who was true in heart and hand,
To the voice of old Columbia, till she wronged his native land!

He buckled on his knapsack—his musket on his breast—
  And donned the plumèd bonnet—sword and pistol by his side;
Then his weeping mother kissed him, and his aged father bless'd,
  And he pinned the floating ribbon to his gallant plume of pride.

And God be with the ribbon, and the floating
plume of pride!
They have gone where duty called them, and may
glory them betide!

He would not soil his honor, and he would not
strike a blow,
  For he loved the aged Union, and he breath'd
no taunting word;
He would dare Columbia, till she swore herself
his foe—
  Forged the chains for freemen—when he
buckled on his sword.
And God be with the freeman, when he buckled
on his sword!
He lives or dies for duty, and he yields no inch
of sward.

The foes they come with thunder, and with blood
and fire arrayed,
  And they swear that we shall own them—they
the masters, we the slaves;
But there's many a gallant laddie, who wears a
blue cockade,
  Will show them what it is to dare the blood
of Southern braves!

And God be with the banner of those gallant
    Southern braves!
They may nobly die as freemen—they can never
    live as slaves!

THE LEGION OF HONOR.

BY H. L. FLASH.

WHY are we forever speaking
    Of the warriors of old?
Men are fighting all around us,
    Full as noble, full as bold.

Ever working, ever striving,
    Mind and muscle, heart and soul,
With the reins of judgment keeping
    Passions under full control.

Noble hearts are beating boldly
    As they ever did on earth;
Swordless heroes are around us,
    Striving ever from their birth.

Tearing down the old abuses,
  Building up the purer laws,
Scattering the dust of ages,
  Searching out the hidden flaws.

Acknowledging no "right divine"
  In kings and princes from the rest;
In their creed he is the noblest
  Who has worked and striven best.

Decorations do not tempt them—
  Diamond stars they laugh to scorn—
Each will wear a "Cross of Honor"
  On the Resurrection morn.

Warriors they in fields of wisdom—
  Like the noble Hebrew youth,
Striking down Goliath's error
  With the God-blessed stone of truth.

Marshaled 'neath the Right's broad banner,
  Forward rush these volunteers,
Beating olden wrong away
  From the fast advancing years.

Contemporaries do not see them,
   But the *coming* times will say
(Speaking of the slandered present),
   "There *were* heroes in that day."

Why are we then idly lying
   On the roses of our life,
While the noble-hearted struggle
   In the world redeeming strife.

Let us rise and join the legion,
   Ever foremost in the fray—
Battling in the name of Progress
   For the nobler, purer day.

"WHAT THE VILLAGE BELL SAID."

BY JOHN M'LEMORE, OF S. C.

FULL many a year in the village church,
   Above the world have I made my home;
And happier there, than if I had hung
   High up in air in a golden dome;
     For I have tolled
     When the slow hearse rolled

Its burden sad to my door;
    And each echo that woke,
    With the solemn stroke,
Was a sigh from the heart of the poor.

I know the great bell of the city spire
  Is a far prouder one than such as I;
And its deafening stroke, compared with mine,
  Is thunder compared with a sigh;
    But the shattering note
    Of his brazen throat,
As it swells on the Sabbath air,
    Far oftener rings
    For other things
Than a call to the house of prayer.

Brave boy, I tolled when your father died,
  And you wept when my tones pealed loud;
And more gently I rung when the lily-white dame
  Your mother dear lay in her shroud:
    And I rang in sweet tone
    The angels might own,
When your sister you gave to your friend;
    Oh! I rang with delight,
    On that sweet summer night,
When they vowed they would love to the end!

But a base foe comes from the regions of crime,
  With a heart all hot with the flames of hell;
And the tones of the bell you have loved so long
  No more on the air shall swell:
    For the people's chief,
    With his proud belief
  That his country's cause is God's own,
    Would change the song,
    The hills have rung
  To the thunder's harsher tone.

Then take me down from the village church,
  Where in peace so long I have hung;
But I charge you, by all the loved and lost,
  Remember the songs I have sung.
    Remember the mound
    Of holy ground
  Where your father and mother lie
    And swear by the love
    For the dead above
  To beat your foul foe, or die.

Then take me; but when (I charge you this)
  You have come to the bloody field,
That the bell of God, to a cannon grown,
  You will ne'er to the foeman yield.

By the love of the past,
Be that hour your last,
When the foe has reached this trust;
And make him a bed
Of patriot dead,
And let him sleep in this holy dust.*

"WE COME! WE COME!"

BY MILLIE MAYFIELD.†

We come! we come for Death or Life,
  For the Grave or Victory!
We come to the broad Red Sea of strife,
  Where the black flag waveth free!
We come as Men, to do or die,
  Nor feel that the lot is hard,
When *our* Hero calls—and our battle-cry
  Is "On, to Beauregard!"

---

* The author of this song was mortally wounded at the battle of Seven Pines.

† Dedicated to the Crescent Regiment, of New Orleans, Col. M. J. Smith.

Up, craven, up! 'tis no time for ease,
   When the crimson war-tide rolls
To our very doors—up, up, for these
   Are times to try men's souls!
The purple gore calls from the sod
   Of our martyred brothers' graves,
And raises a red right hand to God
   To guard our avenging braves.

And unto the last bright drop that thrills
   The depths of the Southern heart,
We must battle for our sunny hills,
   For the freedom of our Mart—
For all that Honor claims, or Right—
   For Country, Love, and Home!
Shout to the trampling steeds of Might
   Our cry—"We come! we come!"

And let our path through their serried ranks
   Be the fierce tornado's track,
That bursts from the torrid's fervid banks
   And scatters destruction black!
For the hot life leaping in the veins
   Of our young Confederacy,
Must break for aye the galling chains
   Of dark-browed Treachery.

On! on! 'tis our gallant chieftain calls
  (He must not call in vain),
For aid to guard his homestead walls—
  Our Hero of the Plain!
We come! we come, to do or die,
  Nor feel that the lot is hard:
"God and our Rights!" be our battle cry,
  And, "On, to Beauregard!"

MANASSAS.

BY A REBEL.

Upon our country's border lay,
Holding the ruthless foe at bay,
Through chilly night and burning day,
  Our army at Manassas.

To them our eager eyes were turned,
While many a restless spirit burned,
And many a fond heart wildly yearned,
  O'er loved ones at Manassas.

For fast the Vandals gathered, strong
In wealth and numbers, all along
Our highways pressed a countless throng,
    To battle at Manassas.

With martial pomp and proud array,
With burnished arms and banners gay,
Panting for the inhuman fray,
    They rolled upon Manassas.

The opening cannons' thunders rent
The air, and ere their charge was spent,
Muskets and rifles quickly sent
    Death to us at Manassas.

But, like a wall of granite, stood
The true, the great, the brave, the good,
Who, firmly holding field and wood,
    Guarded us at Manassas.

They promptly answered fire with fire;
Danger could not with fear inspire
Their hearts, whose courage rose the higher,
    When death ruled at Manassas.

At dawn the murderous work begun;
The battle fiercely raged at noon;
Evening drew on—'twas not done—
    The carnage at Manassas.

Oh, trembling Freedom! didst thou stay
Throughout that agonizing day,
To watch where victory would lay
    Her laurels at Manassas?

Yea! and thy potent trumpet tone
Ordered our gallant warriors on,
To the bold charge which for thee won
    The triumph at Manassas.

Well might the dastard foemen yield,
When Right and Vengeance joined to wield
The well-aimed ball and glittering steel,
    Which hurled them from Manassas.

They broke, and fear lent wings to feet
Flying before our chargers fleet,
Which followed up their wild retreat—
    Their mad rout at Manassas.

Strike! Southrons, strike! for ne'er a foe
So worthy of your every blow
Can your good swords and carbines know,
    As those who sought Manassas.

For that our homes are still secure,
Our wives and sisters still left pure,
Our altars drip not with our gore;
    Thanks, victors of Manassas!

Thy charmèd trumpet sound, O Fame!
Let music catch the loud refrain,
While in a glad, triumphant strain,
    We celebrate Manassas.

And every soldier's breast shall fire
With emulation, and desire
To equal—fame can point no higher—
    The heroes of Manassas.

Alas! that many writhe in pain,
Whose precious blood was spilt to gain
Glory and freedom on thy plain—
    Thy bloody plain, Manassas.

If sympathy can aught avail,
If fervent prayers with Heaven prevail,
In your behalf they shall not fail,
    Poor wounded of Manassas.

Alas! that blended with the tone
Of triumph, breathes the stifled moan
For many brave, whose dear lives won
    The victory of Manassas.

A grateful nation long shall keep
Their memory, and flock to weep
Above the turf where softly sleep
    The martyrs of Manassas.

HANOVER CO., VA., *July 30.*

CHIVALROUS C. S. A.

BY "B."

AIR—"*Vive la Compagnie!*"

I'LL sing you a song of the South's sunny clime,
    Chivalrous C. S. A.!
Which went to house-keeping once on a time;
    Bully for C. S. A.!

Like heroes and princes they lived for awhile,
    Chivalrous C. S. A.!
And routed the Hessians in most gallant style;
    Bully for C. S. A.!
Chorus—Chivalrous, chivalrous people are they!
    Chivalrous, chivalrous people are they!
    In C. S. A.! In C. S. A.!
    Aye, in chivalrous C. S. A.!

They have a bold leader—Jeff. Davis his name—
    Chivalrous C. S. A.!
Good generals and soldiers, all anxious for fame;
    Bully for C. S. A.!
At Manassas they met the North in its pride,
    Chivalrous C. S. A.!
But they easily put McDowell aside;
    Bully for C. S. A.!
    Chorus—Chivalrous, chivalrous people, etc.

Ministers to England and France, it appears,
    Have gone from the C. S. A.!
Who've given the North many fleas in its ears;
    Bully for C. S. A.!
Reminders are being to Washington sent,
    By the chivalrous C. S. A.!

That'll force Uncle Abe full soon to repent;
>   Bully for C. S. A.!
> *Chorus*—Chivalrous, chivalrous people, etc.

Oh, they have the finest of musical ears,
>   Chivalrous C. S. A.!
Yankee Doodle's too vulgar for them, it appears;
>   Bully for C. S. A.!
The North may sing it and whistle it still,
>   Miserable U. S. A.!
Three cheers for the South!—now, boys, with a will!
>   And groans for the U. S. A.!
> *Chorus*—Chivalrous, chivalrous people, etc.

THE BATTLE-FIELD OF MANASSAS.

BY M. F. BIGNEY.

FILL, fill the trump of fame
With the name—
>   MANASSAS—the battle-field of pride;

Where Freedom's heroes fought with their spirits
    all aflame,
Where the Gospel of Liberty was sounded with
    acclaim,
    Where heroes for Liberty have died!

    Come, Fancy, once again
    Fill the plain with armèd men;
Let us see the struggling hosts of Wrong and
    Right;
    Let the tide of battle pour,
    Fight and conquer o'er and o'er,
Till we glow with inspiration at the sight.

    There's glory in the air:
        Everywhere
    Glory rises from the ground,
        All around.
    A hundred thousand men,
    Gather in from hill and glen,
And for battle fierce and bloody they are bound.

    See, see the cohorts come,
    To the sound of fife and drum;
They're the foemen of the North
        Coming forth,

  In the pride of conscious might;
  They would trample down the Right,
As forth they come, those foemen of the North.

  The flag which they bear
   Is a snare:
Its Stripes writhe as snakes upon the air;
  And its Stars, no longer bright,
  Tell of chaos and of night,
   And of how they yet
    Will set
   In despair.

  On comes the lengthening line,
  As if eager for the wine
Which from the press of battle freely flows;
  And from the Southern heart
  Such wine will freely start,
As the pledge to each hecatomb of foes.

  On comes the lengthened line,
  And a "higher law" *divine;*
The snakes on their banners seem to hiss;
  "Destruction to the South,"
  Bursts in hate from every mouth,
And the demon-words are held akin to bliss.

THE BATTLE-FIELD OF MANASSAS.

A brave, heroic band,
    Hand to hand,
To meet the shock of battle are prepared;
    For wife and child they stand—
    For home and native land;
Oh, pray that every hero may be spared!

The drum and fife may sound,
    But their stirring notes are drowned
In the roar and the thunder of the guns;
    The death-charged bullets fly,
    And the shells ascend the sky—
They are offerings to God's and Freedom's sons.

Where Freedom nerves the arm,
    There's a charm;
Where Freedom stirs the heart,
    Fears depart.
    Oh, sacred is the strife,
    And the sacrifice of life,
Where Freedom's chosen heroes point the dart.

God! how the freemen press!
    There's distress
In each lead and iron shower that they send;

Their countless columns pour,
Like the waves in wild uproar,
Beating on a rocky shore
    They would rend.

But firm as rocks our band
    Grandly stand—
For home and native land
    Hand to hand.
How the proud invaders reel,
As with shot and shell and steel,
Destruction wide we deal,
    Sternly grand!

Again, and yet again,
These wild, fanatic men—
Those foemen that invade our Southern homes—
    Still rally to the cry:
    "We must conquer here, or die!
The laurel, or the fate of hellish gnomes!"

Again, and yet again,
    Southern men
Force the fierce insulting foe to retire.
    Again the Northmen fall,
    And to Heaven vainly call,

                    While they yell,
                    "There is hell
                In Southern fire!"

Speed, Beauregard the brave, onward speed!
Speed, Davis unto Johnson, in his need!
        Hurrah! the foemen fly!
        Send the victor shout on high,
For Heaven still rewards the daring deed.

        How fearfully they bleed—
                Man and steed!
        Oh, how their dying prayer
                Rends the air!
        All this for Northern greed,
        All that strange, fanatic creed,
        Which so wickedly they heed.
            Do not spare!

        "The Southron is accurst"—
                So they say;
        "He's baser than the worst
                Beast of prey;"
        And the African is white,
        In those Northern foemen's sight,
As the lily, when it greets the god of day.

Then drive them to their lair;
    Do not spare!
Let shot and shell reply
    To their cry.
Though their bodies taint the air,
And become the vulture's fare,
It is just that such invading hordes should die.

McDowell, in the van,
    Sees his beaten columns fly!
He calls on God and man
    For the aid that both deny;
The army he would rally, as it runs.
Thus, thus, McDowell raves:
"Know ye not, ye unworthy knaves,
That you fight the fight for slaves—
    Sable ones;
Come, and purchase redder graves
    With your guns."

But the guns are thrown away,
The invaders will not stay;
To them a fearful lesson has been read:
For miles strewn all around,
Encrimsoning the rich ground,
Lie their fallen friends—the wounded and the dead.

THE BATTLE-FIELD OF MANASSAS.

    The sun slopes down the west,
    But the foe in wild unrest
Rushes on, though destruction follows fast.
    The Southern cavalcade
    Dyes with red each trusty blade,
And the carnage is terrible and vast!

    Oh, where is Scott, the chief?
    Why brings he not relief?
And Patterson, the tardy, where is he?
    And where is Abe, the Great,
    With his cap and cloak of state?
        He should see
How his warriors can flee.

    Fear lendeth speed to flight,
    And the foe invokes the night
To let its starless curtain quickly fall;
    But it falleth all too slow,
    For the terrors of the foe,
And it seems to them the shadow of a pall.

    A Nemesis concealed
    In the shades of wold and field,
Breathes of vengeance to the foemen as they run;

They are rushing in despair,
But there's carnage everywhere,
And they know not what to welcome or to shun.

    Ten thousand of their slain
        Strew the plain;
The shrieks from ten thousand more arise;
        And the ghosts
        From their hosts
Wail despairingly and vain,
        In their pain,
For a welcome to the skies.

    At morning, in their pride,
        Side by side,
They went forth in their might
        To the fight;
And now they flee in fear,
Trembling like the stricken deer,
At the saber and the spear—
        It is night.

    They came forth to destroy,
With a fierce, fanatic joy,

And boasted of the Rebels they would slay;
   But, ere the set of sun,
   There are hundreds chased by one,
And they pray their legs to bear them safe away.

   For miles strewn all around
      O'er the ground,
   The records of their flight
      Meet the sight:
   Bodies 'neath the horses' tread;
   Bodies living; bodies dead;
And the swords and guns most beautifully bright!

   But let us leave the foe
      In their woe.
To the God of Peace and Battle let us go.
   Let us praise the King of Kings,
   'Neath whose wide-expanded wings
There is shelter for his children here below.
   His arm, unseen, uprears
      Freedom's spears;
   If Freedom's voice be weak,
      His will speak

In the cannon's thunder tones,
Though the answer be in groans,
And though a thousand tyrant hearts may break.

THE SOLDIER'S HEART.

BY F. P. BEAUFORT.

The trumpet calls, and I must go
To meet the vile, invading foe;
But listen, dearest, ere we part—
Thou hast, thou hast the soldier's heart!

It could not be so true to thee
Were it not true to liberty;
Far rather fill a soldier's grave
Than live a dastard and a slave!

Thine eyes shall light dark danger's path,
The gloomy camp, the foeman's wrath;
Above the battle's fiery storm,
I shall behold thy beauteous form!

With thoughts of thee, for thy dear sake,
Redoubled efforts I will make;
And strike with an avenging hand
For lady-love and native land!

Then fare thee well, the trumpet's sound
Commands me to the battle ground;
But listen, dearest, ere we part—
Thou hast, thou hast the soldier's heart.

CONFEDERATE SONG.

AIR—"*Bruce's Address.*"

Written for and dedicated to the Kirk's Ferry Rangers, by their Captain, E. Lloyd Wailes. Sung by the Glee Club on the 4th of July, 1861, at the Kirk's Ferry barbecue (Catahoula, La.), after the presentation of a flag, by the ladies, to the Kirk's Ferry Rangers.

RALLY round our country's flag!
Rally, boys, haste! do not lag;
Come from every vale and crag,
    Sons of liberty!

Northern Vandals tread our soil,
Forth they come for blood and spoil,
To the homes we've gained with toil,
    Shouting, "Slavery!"

Traitorous Lincoln's bloody band
Now invades the freeman's land,
Armed with sword and firebrand,
    'Gainst the brave and free.

Arm ye then for fray and fight,
March ye forth both day and night,
Stop not till the foe's in sight,
    Sons of chivalry.

In your veins the blood still flows
Of brave men who once arose—
Burst the shackles of their foes;
    Honest men and free.

Rise, then, in your power and might,
Seek the spoiler, brave the fight;
Strike for God, for Truth, for Right:
    Strike for Liberty!

SOUTHERN SONG.

BY M. C. FREER.

Tune—"*Wait for the Wagon.*"

Come, all ye sons of freedom,
  And join our Southern band,
We are going to fight the Yankees,
  And drive them from our land.
Justice is our motto,
  And Providence our guide,
So jump into the wagon,
  And we'll all take a ride.
    Chorus—So wait for the wagon, the
      dissolution wagon;
    The South is the wagon, and we'll all
      take a ride.

Secession is our watchword;
  Our rights we all demand;
To defend our homes and firesides
  We pledge our hearts and hands.
Jeff. Davis is our President,

With Stephens by his side;
Great Beauregard our General;
  He joins us in our ride.
    Chorus—So wait for the wagon, etc.

Our wagon is the very best;
  The running gear is good;
Stuffed round the sides with cotton,
  And made of Southern wood.
Carolina is the driver,
  With Georgia by her side;
Virginia holds the flag up,
  While we all take a ride.
    Chorus—So wait for the wagon, etc.

The invading tribe, called Yankees,
  With Lincoln for their guide,
Tried to keep Kentucky
  From joining in the ride;
But she heeded not their entreaties—
  She has come into the ring;
She wouldn't fight for a government
  Where cotton wasn't king.
    Chorus—So wait for the wagon, etc.

Old Lincoln and his Congressmen,
  With Seward by his side,
Put old Scott in the wagon,
  Just for to take a ride.
McDowell was the driver,
  To cross Bull Run he tried,
But there he left the wagon
  For Beauregard to ride.
    Chorus—So wait for the wagon, etc.

Manassas was the battle-ground;
  The field was fair and wide;
The Yankees thought they'd whip us out,
  And on to Richmond ride;
But when they met our "Dixie" boys,
  Their danger they espied;
They wheeled about for Washington,
  And didn't wait to ride.
    Chorus—So wait for the wagon, etc.

Brave Beauregard, God bless him!
  Led legions in his stead,
While Johnson seized the colors
  And waved them o'er his head.

To rising generations,
　　With pleasure we will tell
How bravely our Fisher
　　And gallant Johnson fell.
　　　Chorus—So wait for the wagon, etc.*

MY WIFE AND CHILD.

BY GEN. HENRY R. JACKSON, OF GEORGIA.

The tattoo beats, the lights are gone,
　　The camp around in slumber lies;
The night with solemn pace moves on,
　　And sad, uneasy thoughts arise.
I think of thee, oh, dearest one!
　　Whose love my early life has blest;
Of thee and him, our baby son,
　　Who slumbers on thy gentle breast.

---

*These verses were published, early in 1862, in the Raleigh (N. C.) "Register." From the camp of the Massachusetts Twenty-Second Regiment, they were sent as a part of a letter to the "Boston Traveller," on May 31st, of the same year, and printed in that paper on the 6th of June.

MY WIFE AND CHILD.

God of the tender, hover near
   To her whose watchful eye is wet;
The mother, wife—the doubly dear—
   And cheer her drooping spirits yet.
Now, while she kneels before thy throne,
   Oh, teach her, Ruler of the Skies!
No tear is wept to thee unknown,
   No hair is lost, no sparrow dies.

That thou canst stay the ruthless hand
   Of dark disease, and soothe its pain;
That only by thy stern command
   The battle's lost, the soldier's slain.
By day, by night—in joy or woe—
   By fear oppressed, or hopes beguiled,
From every danger, every foe,
   Oh, God! protect my wife and child!

THE SOUTH IS UP.

BY P. E. C.

The South is up in stern array—
   Chasseurs and Zouaves and Gallic Guard—
Types of their veteran fathers gray,
   Of war-marked visage, saber-scarred—
The children of Marengo's plains,
   Of Austerlitz and Waterloo,
When tyrants dare to speak of chains
   We'll do as their brave sires would do.
The sturdy German, hardy Pole,
   Who knows how Kosciusko fell—
The Tyrolean, who feels his soul
   Fired with that spark which gave them Tell.

The South is up! Italia's sons—
   A Garibaldi in each form—
Their hands are grasping freemen's guns,
   Their bosoms feel his valor warm;
Their crimson shirts, in bloody fields,
   Like walls of flame shall front the foeman;
In that dread hour whoever yields,
   'Tis not the offspring of the Roman;

No renegade, to scorn his brother
While guarding their adopted mother—
One feeling, *nationale* and grand,
Still binds them to their native land.

The South is up! those brawny hands
  That bless in peace or crush in war,
Who fought on India's burning sands,
  At Egypt's Nile, and Trafalgar;
That reckless mirth, that fiery joy,
  On field, or fort, or slippery deck,
From Clontarf's plains to Fontenoy,
  At Quatre Bras or old Quebec;
Magenta, Malakoff, Redan,
  Has heard their Celtic "Clear the way!"
The slandered, exiled Irishman
  Stands for his Southern home to-day;
And when, perchance, in Death's eclipse
  He grasps her flag with 'legiance due,
The last breath lingering on his lips
  Might proudly say, I'm Irish, too!

The South is up! her native sons,
  Whose spirit prompts them to be free,
Spring forth to man their trophied guns,
  So bravely won at Monterey—

Surpassing Buena Vista's deeds,
  Or Palo Alto's feats again,
Though wives be wreathed in widow's weeds
  And children weep for fathers slain.
What! think to bind the South? 'Tis vain!
  Freedom's inheritors at birth,
Not all the leagued infernal train,
  If they were mustered here on earth,
Those flashing eyes, like gleaming steel,
  Those hero boys and veterans gray!
Oh, yes! the throbbing heart can feel—
  The South is up in stern array.

Yet sad 'twill grieve the Southern heart
  To meet their brethren foot to foot,
But cancers on a vital part
  Must now be severed branch and root;
They share with us a blood-bought fame
  From foreign foe and savage grim;
The memory of our George's name,
  Revered by us, is dear to them;
Our ships in every clime have shown,
  Where jealous monarchies might see,
What stars upon our flag have grown
  From old *thirteen* to *thirty-three*;

Soldier to lead, or sage to teach,
  Deep-scienced minds, of knowledge vast,
The great one's fame, as in a niche,
  Lives in the history of the past.
Now, pausing o'er our doubtful fate
  We *have been*, or we *shall be*, great.

THE OLD RIFLEMAN.

BY FRANK TICKNOR, M. D.

Now, bring me out my buckskin suit!
  My pouch and powder, too!
We'll see if seventy-six can shoot
  As sixteen used to do.

Old Bess! we've kept our barrels bright!
  Our triggers quick and true!
As far, if not as *fine* a sight,
  As long ago, we drew!

And pick me out a trusty flint!
  A real white and blue;
Perhaps 'twill win the *other* tint,
  Before the hunt is through!

Give boys your brass percussion-caps!
  Old "shut-pan" suits as well!
There's something in the *sparks;* perhaps
  There's something in the smell!

We've seen the red-coat Briton bleed!
  The red-skin Indian, too!
We never thought to draw a bead
  On Yankee-doodle-doo!

But, Bessie! bless your dear old heart!
  Those days are mostly done;
And now we must revive the art
  Of shooting on the run!

If Doodle must be meddling, why,
  There's only this to do:
Select the black spot in his eye
  And let the daylight through!

And if he doesn't like the way
  That Bess presents the view,
He'll, maybe, change his mind and stay
  Where the good Doodles do!

Where Lincoln lives. The man, you know,
  Who kissed the Testament ;
To keep the Constitution ? No !
To keep the Government!

We'll hunt for Lincoln, Bess ! old tool,
  And take him half and half ;
We'll aim to *hit* him, if a fool,
  And *miss* him if a calf !

We'll teach these shot-gun boys the tricks
  By which a war is won ;
Especially how seventy-six
  Took Tories on the run.

ONLY ONE KILLED.

BY JULIA L. KEYES.

ONLY one killed in Company B,
  'Twas a trifling loss—one man !
A charge of the bold and dashing Lee,
While merry enough it was, to see
  The enemy, as he ran.

Only one killed upon our side—
　Once more to the field they turn.
Quietly now the horsemen ride,
And pause by the form of the one who died,
　So bravely, as now we learn.

Their grief for the comrade loved and true
　For a time was unconcealed;
They saw the bullet had pierced him through;
That his pain was brief—ah! very few
　Die thus on the battle-field.

The news has gone to his home, afar—
　Of the short and gallant fight;
Of the noble deeds of the young La Var,
Whose life went out as a falling star
　In the skirmish of the night.

"Only one killed! It was my son,"
　The widowed mother cried;
She turned but to clasp the sinking one,
Who heard not the words of the victory won,
　But of him who had bravely died.

Ah! death to her were a sweet relief,
　The bride of a single year.

Oh! would she might, with her weight of grief,
Lie down in the dust, with the autumn leaf,
  Now trodden and brown and sere!

But no, she must bear through coming life
  Her burden of silent woe,
The aged mother and youthful wife
Must live through a nation's bloody strife,
  Sighing and waiting to go.

Where the loved are meeting beyond the stars,
  Are meeting no more to part,
They can smile once more through the crystal
    bars—
Where never more will the woe of wars
  O'ershadow the loving heart.

THE WAR CHRISTIAN'S THANKSGIVING.

Respectfully dedicated to the War Clergy of the United States.

BY GEORGE H. MILES, OF BALTIMORE.

Oh, God of battles! once again,
  With banner, trump and drum,
And garments in thy wine-press dyed,
  To give Thee thanks we come.

No goats or bullocks garlanded,
   Unto Thine altars go;
With brother's blood, by brothers shed,
   Our glad libations flow.

From pest-house and from dungeon foul,
   Where, maimed and torn, they die,
From gory trench and charnel-house,
   Where, heap on heap, they lie.

In every groan that yields a soul,
   Each shriek a heart that rends,
With every breath of tainted air,
   Our homage, Lord, ascends.

We thank Thee for the saber's gash,
   The cannon's havoc wild;
We bless Thee for the widow's tears,
   The want that starves her child!

We give Thee praise that Thou hast lit
   The torch and fanned the flame;
That lust and rapine hunt their prey,
   Kind Father, in Thy name!

That for the songs of idle joy
  False angels sang of yore,
Thou sendest war on earth—ill-will
  To men for evermore!

We know that wisdom, truth and right
  To us and ours are given;
That Thou hast clothed us with the wrath,
  To do the work of heaven.

We know that plains and cities waste
  Are pleasant in Thine eyes—
Thou lov'st a hearthstone desolate,
  Thou lov'st a mourner's cries.

Let not our weakness fall below
  The measure of Thy will,
And while the press hath wine to bleed,
  Oh, tread it with us still!

Teach us to hate—as Jesus taught
  Fond fools, of yore, to love;
Give us Thy vengeance as our own—
  Thy pity, hide above!

Teach us to turn, with reeking hands,
  The pages of Thy word,
And learn the blessed curses there,
  On them that sheathe the sword.

Where'er we tread may deserts spring,
  Till none are left to slay ;
And when the last red-drop is shed,
  We'll kneel again—and pray !

UP! UP! LET THE STARS OF OUR BANNER.

BY M. F. BIGNEY.

Respectfully dedicated to the Soldiers of the South.

Up! up! Let the stars of our banner
  Flash out like the brilliants above!
Beneath them we'll shield from dishonor
  The homes and the dear ones we love.
    With "God and our Right!"
    Our cry in the fight,

We'll drive the invader afar,
And we'll carve out a name
In the temple of Fame
With the weapons of glorious war.

Arise with an earnest endeavor—
A nation shall hallow the deed;
The foe must be silenced forever,
Though millions in battle may bleed.
With "God and our Right!" etc.

Strong arms and a conquerless spirit
We bring as our glory and guard:
If courage a triumph can merit,
Then Freedom shall be our reward.
With "God and our Right!" etc.

Beneath the high sanction of Heaven,
We'll fight as our forefathers fought;
Then pray that to us may be given
Such guerdon as fell to their lot.
With "God and our Right!" etc.

THE SOLDIER BOY.

BY H. M. L.

I give my soldier boy a blade,
  In fair Damascus fashioned well;
Who first the glittering falchion swayed,
  Who first beneath its fury fell,
I know not: but I hope to know
  That for no mean or hireling trade,
To guard no feeling, base or low,
  I give my soldier boy a blade.

Cool, calm, and clear, the lucid flood,
  In which its tempering work was done;
As calm, as clear, as clear of mood
  Be thou whene'er it sees the sun;
For country's claim, at honor's call,
  For outraged friend, insulted maid,
At mercy's voice to bid it fall,
  I give my soldier boy a blade.

The eye which marked its peerless edge,
  The hand that weighed its balanced poise,
Anvil and pincers, forge and wedge,
  Are gone with all their flame and noise;

 And still the gleaming sword remains.
  So when in dust I low am laid,
 Remember by these heartfelt strains,
  I give my soldier boy a blade.

LYNCHBURG, VA., *May* 18, 1861.

A SOUTHERN GATHERING SONG.

BY L. VIRGINIA FRENCH.

AIR—"*Hail Columbia.*" *

SONS of the South, beware the foe!
Hark to the murmur deep and low,
Rolling up like the coming storm,
Swelling up like sounding storm,
 Hoarse as the hurricanes that brood
 In space's far infinitude!
Minute guns of omen boom
Through the future's folded gloom;

---

 * A good clergyman, on being censured for introducing a "song tune" into his choir at church, replied that he "did not think it fair that the devil should have all the good music." In like manner, we will *never* give up "Hail Columbia" to the Abolitionists. It is *ours;* and we mean to hold, as one of our dearest rights, this, the grandest march ever composed by mortal man.

Sounds prophetic fill the air,
Heed the warning—and prepare!
 Watch! be wary—every hour
 Mark the foeman's gathering power—
 Keep watch and ward upon his track
 And crush the rash invader back!

Sons of the brave!—a barrier stanch
Breasting the alien avalanche—
Manning the battlements of RIGHT;
Up, for your *Country, "God, and right!"*
Form your battalions steadily,
And strike for death or victory!
Surging onward sweeps the wave,
Serried columns of the brave,
Banded 'neath the benison
Of Freedom's godlike Washington!
 Stand! but should the invading foe
 Aspire to lay your altars low,
 Charge on the tyrant ere he gain
 Your iron arteried domain!

Sons of the brave! when tumult trod
The tide of revolution—God

Looked from His throne on "the things of
   time,"
And two new stars in the reign of time
He bade to burn in the azure dome—
The freeman's LOVE and the freeman's HOME!
Holy of Holies! guard them well,
Baffle the despot's secret spell,
And let the chords of life be riven
Ere you yield those gifts of Heaven!
  Io pæan! trumpet notes
    Shake the air where our banner floats;
  Io triumphe! still we see
    The land of the South is the home of the free!

BATTLE-CALL.

Nec temere, nec timide.

Dedicated to her Countrymen, the Cavaliers of the South,

BY ANNIE CHAMBERS KETCHUM.

GENTLEMEN of the South!
  Gird on your flashing swords!
Darkly along your borders fair
  Gather the ruffian hordes!

Ruthless and fierce they come;
  Even at the cannon's mouth
To blast the glory of your land,
  Gentlemen of the South!

Ride forth in your stately pride,
  Each bearing on his shield
Ensigns your fathers won of yore
  On many a well-fought field.
Let this be your battle-cry,
  Even to the cannon's mouth,
Cor unum via una! Onward!
  Gentlemen of the South!

Brave knights of a knightly race,
  Gordon and Chambers and Gray,
Show to the minions of the North
  How valor dares the fray!
Let them read on each spotless crest,
  Even at the cannon's mouth,
Decori decus addit avito,
  Gentlemen of the South!

Morrison, Douglas, Stuart,
  Erskine and Bradford and West,

Your gauntlets on many a hill and plain
   Have stood the battle's test.
Animo non astutia!
   March to the cannon's mouth,
Heirs of the brave dead centuries,
   Gentlemen of the South!

Call out your stalwart men,
   Workers in brass and steel,
Bid the swart artisans come forth
   At sound of the trumpet's peal;
Give them your war-cry, Erskine,
   Fight to the cannon's mouth—
Bid the men *forward*, Douglas, forward!
   Yeomanry of the South!

Brave hunters, ye have met
   The fierce black bear in the fray,
Ye have trailed the panther night by night,
   Ye have chased the fox by day;
Your prancing chargers pant
   To dash at the gray wolf's mouth,
Your arms are sure of their quarry—forward!
   Gentlemen of the South!

Fight! that the lowly serf
   And the high-born lady, still
May bide in their proud dependency,
   Free subjects of your will;
Teach the base North how ill—
   At the belching cannon's mouth—
He fares who touches your household gods,
   Gentlemen of the South!

From mother, and wife, and child,
   From faithful and happy slave,
Prayers for your sake ascend to Him
   Whose arm is strong to save.
We check the gathering tears,
   Though ye go to the cannon's mouth;
Dominus providebit! Onward!
   Gentlemen of the South!

DUNROBIN COTTAGE.

THE BONNIE BLUE FLAG.

BY HARRY MACARTHY.

We are a band of brothers, and natives to the soil,
Fighting for the property we gained by honest toil,
And when our rights were threatened, the cry rose near and far:
Hurrah for the bonnie Blue Flag that bears a single star!
Chorus—Hurrah! hurrah! for the bonnie Blue Flag
    That bears a single star.

As long as the Union was faithful to her trust,
Like friends and like brothers, kind were we and just;
But now when Northern treachery attempts our rights to mar,
We hoist on high the bonnie Blue Flag that bears a single star.

First, gallant South Carolina nobly made the stand;
Then came Alabama, who took her by the hand;

Next, quickly, Mississippi, Georgia, and Florida—
All raised the flag, the bonnie Blue Flag that bears a single star.

Ye men of valor, gather round the banner of the right;
Texas and fair Louisiana join us in the fight.
Davis, our loved President, and Stephens, statesmen are;
Now rally round the bonnie Blue Flag that bears a single star.

And here's to brave Virginia! the Old Dominion State
With the young Confederacy at length has linked her fate.
Impelled by her example, now other States prepare
To hoist on high the bonnie Blue Flag that bears a single star.

Then here's to our Confederacy; strong we are and brave,
Like patriots of old we'll fight, our heritage to save;
And rather than submit to shame, to die we would prefer;
So cheer for the bonnie Blue Flag that bears a single star.

Then cheer, boys, cheer, raise the joyous shout,
For Arkansas and North Carolina now have both
    gone out;
And let another rousing cheer for Tennessee be
    given,
The single star of the bonnie Blue Flag has
    grown to be eleven!

THE BATTLE AT BULL RUN.

BY RUTH.

FORWARD, my brave columns, forward!
No other word was spoken;
But in the quick and mighty rustling of their feet,
And in the flashing of their eyes, 'twas proved
This was enough.
Men, whose *every* bosom had a *noble* heart,
And who had left their homes, their sacred *rights*
To gain: To *these* this was no trying hour,
No time to waver, and to doubt. But one,
For which they'd hoped and prayed—
One (as they felt) they'd brought not on
Themselves, but which they knew *must come*—

And *nobly, O most nobly,* did their
Bravery, their *sense* of *right,* sustain them.

And Lincoln's hordes—
They knew *not* with what natures they contended,
Seemed not to feel their *motives* differed, as
Does heaven from earth.
They, the poor, miserable, *hired* outcasts, whose
Principles were bought,
And men, whose courage, bravery, and noble aims,
Had come to be, throughout the land,
A proverb.

And *what* the end?
What *could,* what *should it be,* than what it *was?*
A *brilliant, glorious* VICTORY.

The South weeps o'er her slain:
And well she may; for they were jewels
From her diadem.
She weeps; sheds tears of grief, of sorrow,
And of PRIDE.

    LOUISVILLE, KY., *July* 24, 1861.

THE SOUTHRON MOTHER'S CHARGE.

BY THOMAS B. HOOD.

You go, my son, to the battle-field,
   To repel the invading foe;
Mid its fiercest conflicts *never* yield
   Till death shall lay you low.

Our God, who smiles upon the Right
   And frowns upon the Wrong,
Will nerve you for our holy fight,
   And make your courage strong.

Our cause is just, for it we pray
   At morning, noon, and night,
Upon our banners we inscribe,
   God, Liberty, and Right.

I love you as I love my life,
   You are my only son;
Your country calls, go forth and fight
   Till Freedom's cause is won.

It may be that you fall in death,
   Contending for your home,
Yet your aged mother will not be
   Forsaken though alone.

A thousand generous hearts there are
  Throughout this sunny land,
Whose ample fortunes will be spent
  With an unsparing hand.

Now go, my son, a mother's prayers
  Will ever follow thee;
And in the thickest of the fight
  Strike home for liberty!

On every hill, in every glen,
  We'll fight till we are free;
We'll fight till every limpid brook
  Runs crimson to the sea.

No truce we know, till every foe
  Shall leave our hallowed sod,
And we regain that heaven-born boon,
  "Freedom to worship God."

NEW ORLEANS, LA.

OUR BOYS ARE GONE.

BY COL. HAMILTON WASHINGTON.

Our boys are gone 'till the war is o'er,
   In the ranks of death you'll find them;
With duty's path of blood before,
   And with all they love behind them:
They bear our hearts to the tented field—
   Each danger makes them dearer—
Their faithful hearts our only shield
   From the foe still drawing nearer.

With pride we hear of the perils braved
   And the wreaths they win of glory;
With joy we hear of lov'd ones saved
   From each field of battle gory;
And joy is mix'd with fleeting pain
   As we look to Heaven o'er us,
And think that there we'll meet again,
   With the brave who've gone before us.

THE SOUTHERN PLEIADES.

BY LAURA LORRIMER.

When first our Southern flag arose,
   Beside the heaving sea,
It bore upon its silken folds
   A green Palmetto tree.
All honor to that banner brave,
   It roused the blood of yore,
And nerved the arm of Southern men
   For valiant deeds once more.

When storm clouds darkened o'er our sky,
   That star, the first of seven,
Shone out amid the mist and gloom,
   To light our country's heaven.
The glorious seven! long may their flag
   Wave proudly on the breeze;
Long may they burn on fame's broad sky—
   The Southern Pleiades!

Nashville Patriot.

THE STARS AND BARS.

BY A. J. REQUIER.

FLING wide the dauntless banner
  To every Southern breeze,
Baptized in flame, with Sumter's name—
A patriot and a hero's fame—
  From Moultrie to the seas!
That it may cleave the morning sun
  And, streaming, sweep the night,
The emblem of a battle won
  With Yankee ships in sight.

Come, hucksters, from your markets,
  Come, bigots, from your caves,
Come, venal spies, with brazen lies
Bewildering your deluded eyes,
  That we may dig your graves;
Come, creatures of a sordid clown
  And driveling traitor's breath,
A single blast shall blow you down
  Upon the fields of Death.

The very flag you carry
  Caught its reflected grace,

In fierce alarms, from Southern arms,
When foemen threatened all your farms,
  And never saw your face;
Ho! braggarts of New England's shore,
  Back to your hills and delve
The soil whose craven sons foreswore
  The flag in eighteen-twelve!

We wreathed around the roses
  It wears before the world,
And made it bright with storied light,
In every scene of bloody fight
  Where it has been unfurled;
And think ye, now, the dastard hands
  That never yet could hold
Its staff, shall wave it o'er our lands,
  To glut the greed of gold?

No! by the truth of Heaven
  And its eternal Sun,
By every sire whose altar fire
Burns on to beckon and inspire,
  It never shall be done;
Before that day the kites shall wheel
  Hail-thick on Northern heights,

And there our bared, aggressive steel
  Shall countersign our rights!

Then spread the flaming banner
  O'er mountain, lake, and plain,
Before its bars, degraded Mars
Has kissed the dust with all his stars,
  And will be struck again;
For could its triumph now be stayed
  By Hell's prevailing gates,
A sceptred Union would be made
  The grave of sovereign States.

THE MARCH.

BY JOHN W. OVERALL.

Tramp, tramp, tramp, tramp!
  Go the Southern braves to battle,
How they shine, each gleaming line!
  Flashing sabers! how they rattle!
Every lip is now compressed,
  Every heart now yearns for glory,
Every eye with patriot fire
  Burns for battle fierce and gory!

Tramp, tramp, tramp, tramp!
  Death is in each hidden saber,
Reaper of the fields of Time,
  Look ye for a giant's labor!
How sublime! when patriots feel
  All the strength of self-reliance,
Marching on to meet the foe,
  With a stern and grim defiance!

See how proudly floats our flag!
  White! our cause is pure and grand, man!
Red! a living flood shall flow
  From every foe now in the land, man!
Blue! aye, heaven's stars are there!
  Sparkling in their azure beauty!
Tramp, tramp, tramp, tramp!
  Go the messengers of duty!

SOUTHERN WAR SONG.

BY N. P. W.

To horse! to horse! our standard flies,
  The bugles sound the call;
An alien navy stems our seas—

The voice of battle's on the breeze,
   Arouse ye, one and all!

From beauteous Southern homes we come,
   A band of brothers true—
Resolved to fight for liberty,
And live or perish with our flag—
   The noble Red and Blue.

Though tamely crouch to Northern frown
   Kentucky's tardy train;
Though invaded soil Maryland mourns,
Though brave Missouri vainly spurns,
   And foaming gnaws the chain;

Oh! had they marked the avenging call
   Their brethren's insults gave,
Disunion ne'er their ranks had mown,
Nor patriot valor, desperate grown,
   Sought freedom in the grave;

Shall we, too, bend the stubborn head,
   In Freedom's temple born—
Dress our pale cheek in timid smiles,
To hail a master in our house,
   Or brook a victor's scorn?

No! though destruction o'er the land
   Come pouring as a flood,
The sun that sees our falling day,
Shall mark our saber's deadly sway,
   And set that night in blood!

For gold let Northern legions fight,
   Or plunder's bloody gain;
Unbribed, unbought, our swords we draw,
To guard our homes, to fence our law,
   Nor shall their edge be vain.

And now that breath of Northern gale
   Has fanned the Stars and Bars,
And footstep of invader rude,
With rapine foul, and red with blood,
   Us rights and liberty debars.

Then farewell home, and farewell friends,
   Adieu each tender tie,
Resolved we mingle in the tide,
Where charging squadrons furious ride,
   To conquer or to die.

To horse, to horse! the sabers gleam,
   High sounds our bugle-call,

Combined by honor's sacred tie,
Our word is, Rights and Liberty!
March forward, one and all!

Louisville Courier.

WE'LL BE FREE IN MARYLAND.

BY ROBERT E. HOLTZ.

Air—"*Gideon's Band.*"

THE boys down South in Dixie's land,
The boys down South in Dixie's land,
The boys down South in Dixie's land,
Will come and rescue Maryland.
Chorus—If you will join the Dixie band,
    Here's my heart and here's my hand,
    If you will join the Dixie band;
    We're fighting for a home.

The Northern foes have trod us down,
The Northern foes have trod us down,
The Northern foes have trod us down,
But we will rise with true renown.
    If you will join the Dixie band, etc.

The tyrants they must leave our door,
The tyrants they must leave our door,
The tyrants they must leave our door,
Then we'll be free in Baltimore.
    If you will join the Dixie band, etc.

These hirelings they'll never stand,
These hirelings they'll never stand,
These hirelings they'll never stand,
Whenever they see the Southern band.
    If you will join the Dixie band, etc.

Old Abe has got into a trap,
Old Abe has got into a trap,
Old Abe has got into a trap,
And he can't get out with his Scotch cap.
    If you will join the Dixie band, etc.

Nobody's hurt is easy spun,
Nobody's hurt is easy spun,
Nobody's hurt is easy spun,
But the Yankees caught it at Bull Run.
    If you will join the Dixie band, etc.

We rally to Jeff. Davis true,
Beauregard and Johnston, too,

Magruder, Price, and General Bragg,
And give three cheers for the Southern flag.
   If you will join the Dixie band, etc.

We'll drink this toast to one and all,
Keep cocked and primed for the Southern call,
The day will come, we'll make the stand,
Then we'll be free in Maryland.
   If you will join the Dixie band, etc.

January 30, 1862.

WAR SONG.

BY J. H. WOODCOCK.

Tune—"*Bonnie Blue Flag.*"

Huzza! huzza! let's raise the battle-cry,
   And whip the Yankees from our land,
Or with them fall and die.
   Rush on our Southron columns,
And make the brigands feel
   That all the booty they will get,
Will be our Southron steel.
Huzza! huzza! let's raise (the) our banner high,

And nobly drive the Yankees out,
  Or with them fall and die.

Rush on the columns—let every Southron brave
  Nobly charge the accursèd foe,
Or find a soldier's grave.
  With bowie and with pike,
We'll rally to the field,
  And bravely to the last we'll strike,
Resolved we'll never yield.
  Huzza! huzza! etc.

We are fighting for our mothers, our sisters, and
    our wives;
  For these, and our country's rights,
We'll sacrifice our lives.
  Then, trusting still to Heaven,
We'll charge the invading host,
  Till liberty and independence
Shall be the nation's boast.
  Huzza! huzza! etc.

Then on with our columns—slay the vandal foe—
  Beat them from our sunny soil,
And lay their colors low.
  To the great God of nations

Our sacred cause confide,
  For we are fighting for our liberty,
And He is on our side.
  Huzza! huzza! etc.

A NEW RED, WHITE, AND BLUE.

WRITTEN FOR A LADY, BY JEFF. THOMPSON.

MISSOURI is the pride of the nation,
The hope of the brave and the free;
The Confederacy will furnish the rations,
But the fighting is trusted to thee;
For, brave boys, your soil has been noted,
And your flag has been trusted to you;
For freedom you have not yet voted,
But you fight for the Red, White, and Blue.
  Chorus—Three cheers, etc.

The Stars shall shine bright in the heaven,
But the Stripes should be trailed in the dust,
For they are no longer the sign of the haven
Of the brave, of the free, or the just;

The Bars now in triumph shall wave
O'er the land of the faithful and true;
O'er the home of the Southern brave
Shall float the new Red, White, and Blue.
    Chorus—Three cheers, etc.

O JOHNNY BULL, MY JO JOHN.

AIR—"*John Anderson, my Jo.*"

It was stated in the Richmond "Dispatch" during the last days of December, 1861, that a gentleman, just from the West Indies, had said that there were eighty-seven British ships-of-war lying in those waters. This statement gave rise to the following imitation of an old song:

O JOHNNY Bull, my Jo John! I wonder what you mean,
By sending all these frigates out, commissioned by the Queen;
You'll frighten off the Yankees, John, and why should you do so?
Best catch and sink, or burn them all, O Johnny Bull, my Jo!

O Johnny Bull, my Jo John! when Yankee hands
    profane,
Were laid in wanton insult upon the lion's mane,
He roared so loud and long, John, they quickly
    let him go,
And sank upon their trembling knees, O Johnny
    Bull, my Jo!

O Johnny Bull, my Jo John! when Lincoln first
    began
To try his hand at war, John, you were a peace-
    ful man;
But now your blood is up, John, and well the
    Yankees know,
You play the —— when you start, O Johnny Bull,
    my Jo!

O Johnny Bull, my Jo John, let's take the field
    together,
And hunt the Yankee Doodles home, in spite of
    wind and weather,
And ere a twelvemonth roll around, to Boston
    we will go,
And eat our Christmas dinner there, O Johnny
    Bull, my Jo!

"SOUTHRONS."

BY CATHERINE M. WARFIELD.

You can never win them back—
    Never! never!
Though they perish on the track
    Of your endeavor;
Though their corses strew the earth,
That SMILED upon their birth,
And blood pollutes each hearth-
    Stone forever!

They have risen to a man,
    Stern and fearless;
Of your curses and your ban
    They are careless.
Every hand is on its knife,
Every gun is primed for strife,
Every PALM contains a life,
    High and peerless!

You have no such blood as theirs
    For the shedding:
In the veins of cavaliers
    Was its heading:

You have no such stately men
In your "abolition den,"
To march through foe and fen,
    Nothing dreading!

They may fall before the fire
  Of your legions,
Paid with gold for murderous hire—
  Bought allegiance;
But for every drop you shed,
You shall have a mound of dead,
So that vultures may be fed
    In our regions!

But the battle to the strong
    Is not given,
When the Judge of Right and Wrong
    Sits in heaven;
And the God of David still
    Guides the pebble with *His will;*
There are giants yet to kill—
    Wrongs unshriven!

"NIL DESPERANDUM."

Inscribed to our Soldier-boys,

BY ADA ROSE.

The Yankee hosts are coming,
  With their glittering rows of steel,
And sharp, from many a skirmish,
  Comes the rifle's ringing peal,
Warning you how very near
  The Northern "Hessians" are,
With their overwhelming forces;
  But ne'er must you despair.

For though they come on, surging
  Like a mighty rolling sea,
They're *hired* by their master, "Abe"—
  You fight for *Liberty*.
So bravely you must meet them,
  And face the cannon's blare;
Your watchword, "Victory or Death,"
  And never you despair.

True, the cloud is dark and lowering,
  But behind a cheerful ray,

And the night is always darkest
  Just before the break of day.
Have faith; the cloud will soon disperse,
  For the light is surely there;
The day will soon be dawning,
  So never you despair.

Go, emulate brave Washington,
  Who led a little band,
To drive the proud oppressors
  From off their happy land.
The enemy outnumbered,
  By far, the "rebels" there;
But bravely they encountered them,
  Nor yielded to despair.

'Tis said that "rebel" chieftain,
  Ere they sought the battle's fray,
Would ask our Heavenly Father
  To be their shield and stay;
And then they'd march with confidence,
  Well knowing He'd be there;
And that must be the reason why
  They never did despair.

Likewise, if you will ask Him,
  He'll meet you on the field,
To be a guard about you,
  And your support and shield;
The foe shall fly before you,
  As you shout your victory there;
Then don't forget to plead with Him,
  And never to despair.
    PINE BLUFF, ARK.

ADDRESS OF THE WOMEN TO THE SOUTHERN TROOPS.

BY MRS. J. T. H. CROSS.

AIR—"*Bruce's Address.*"

SOUTHERN men, unsheathe the sword,
Inland and along the board;
Backward drive the Northern horde—
  Rush to Victory!

Let your banners kiss the sky,
Be "The Right" your battle cry!
Be the God of Battles nigh—
  Crown you in the fight!

Pressing back the tears that start,
We behold your hosts depart,
Saying, with heroic heart,
  Clothe your arms with might!

Lower the proud oppressor's crest!
Or, if he should prove the best,
Dead, not dishonored, rest
  On the field of blood!

We—may God so give us grace!—
Sons will rear, to take your place;
Strong the foemen's steel to face—
  Strong in heart and hand!

Death your serried ranks may sweep,
Proud shall be the tears we weep—
Sacredly our hearts shall keep
  Memory of your deeds!

Though our land be left forlorn,
Spirit of the Southron-born
Northern rage shall laugh to scorn—
  Northern hosts defy.

He that last is doomed to die
Shall, with his expiring sigh,
Send aloft the battle-cry,
 "God defend the Right!"

THE CAVALIERS OF DIXIE.

BY BENJAMIN F. PORTER.

Ye Cavaliers of Dixie!
Who guard the Southern shores,
Whose standards brave the battle storm
Which o'er our border roars;
Your glorious sabers draw once more,
And charge the Northern foe;
And reap their columns deep,
Where the raging tempests blow,
And the iron hail in floods descends,
And the bloody torrents flow.

Ye Cavaliers of Dixie!
Though dark the tempest lower,
What arms will wear the tyrants chains,
What dastard heart will cower?

Bright o'er the night a sign shall rise
To lead to victory!
And your swords reap their hordes,
Where the battle tempests blow;
Where the iron hail in floods descends,
And the bloody torrents flow.

The South! she needs no ramparts,
No lofty towers to shield;
Your bosoms are her bulwarks strong,
Breastworks that never yield!
The thunders of your battle blades
Shall sweep the servile foe;
While their gore stains the shore,
Where the battle tempests blow;
Where the iron hail in floods descends,
And the bloody torrents flow.

The battle-flag of Dixie!
With crimson field shall flame,
Her azure cross and silver stars
Shall light her sons to fame!
When peace with olive-branch returns,
That flag's white folds shall glow
Still bright on every height,

When storm has ceased to blow,
And the battle tempests roar no more;
Nor the bloody torrents flow.

Oh ! battle-flag of Dixie !
Long, long, triumphant wave !
Where'er the storms of battle roar,
Or victory crowns the brave !
The Cavaliers of Dixie !
In woman's song shall glow
The fame of your name,
When the storm has ceased to blow,
When the battle tempests rage no more
Nor the bloody torrents flow.*

LAND OF KING COTTON.

BY JO. AUGUSTINE SIGNAIGO.

Air—"*Red, White, and Blue.*"

Oh ! Dixie, the land of King Cotton,
    The home of the brave and the free;

---

* This song was very popular with the Southern troops, and was sung with great effect to the measure of "Ye Mariners of England."

A nation by Freedom begotten,
  The terror of despots to be;
Wherever thy banner is streaming,
  Base tyranny quails at thy feet,
And Liberty's sunlight is beaming,
  In splendor of majesty sweet.
Chorus—Three cheers for our army so true,
  Three cheers for Price, Johnston, and Lee,
  Beauregard, and our Davis, forever;
  The pride of the brave and the free!

When Liberty sounds her war-rattle,
  Demanding her right and her due,
The first land who rallies to battle
  Is Dixie, the shrine of the true;
Thick as leaves of the forest in summer,
  Her brave sons will rise on each plain;
And strike, until each vandal comer
  Lies dead on the soil he would stain.
    Three cheers for our army, etc.

May the names of the dead, that we cherish,
  Fill memory's cup to the brim;
May the laurels they've won never perish,
  Nor "star of their glory grow dim;"

May the States of the South never sever,
  But champions of freedom e'er be;
May they flourish, Confed'rate forever,
  The boast of the brave and the free.
    Three cheers for our army, etc.*

THE GUERILLAS.

BY S. TEACKLE WALLIS.

Awake and to horse, my brothers!
  For the dawn is glimmering gray,
And hark! in the crackling brushwood
  There are feet that tread this way.

"Who cometh?" "A friend." "What tidings?"
  "O God! I sicken to tell;
For the earth seems earth no longer,
  And its sights are sights of hell!

"From the far-off conquered cities
  Comes a voice of stifled wail,

---

*This song was published in the Memphis "Appeal," in December, 1861, was a great favorite with Tennessee troops, and was sung even after the peace was declared.

And the shrieks and moans of the houseless
   Ring out, like a dirge on the gale.

"I've seen from the smoking village
   Our mothers and daughters fly;
I've seen where the little children
   Sank down in the furrows to die.

"On the banks of the battle-stained river
   I stood as the moonlight shone,
And it glared on the face of my brother,
   As the sad wave swept him on.

"Where my home was glad, are ashes,
   And horrors and shame had been there,
For I found on the fallen lintel
   This tress of my wife's torn hair!

"They are turning the slaves upon us,
   And with more than the fiend's worst art,
Have uncovered the fire of the savage,
   That slept in his untaught heart!

"The ties to our hearths that bound him,
   They have rent with curses away,
And maddened him, with their madness,
   To be almost as brutal as they.

"With halter, and torch, and Bible,
  And hymns to the sound of the drum,
They preach the gospel of murder,
  And pray for lust's kingdom to come.

"To saddle! to saddle! my brothers!
  Look up to the rising sun,
And ask of the God who shines there,
  Whether deeds like these shall be done!

"Wherever the vandal cometh,
  Press home to his heart with your steel,
And when at his bosom you can not,
  Like the serpent, go strike at his heel.

"Through thicket and wood, go hunt him,
  Creep up to his camp-fire side,
And let ten of his corpses blacken
  Where one of our brothers hath died.

"In his fainting, foot-sore marches,
  In his flight from the stricken fray,
In the snare of the lonely ambush,
  The debts we owe him, pay.

"In God's hand alone is vengeance,
  But he strikes with the hands of men,
And his blight would wither our manhood,
  If we smite not the smiter again.

"By the graves where our fathers slumber,
  By the shrines where our mothers prayed,
By our homes, and hopes, and freedom,
  Let every man swear on his blade,

"That he will not sheathe nor stay it,
  Till from point to hilt it glow
With the flush of Almighty vengeance,
  In the blood of the felon foe."

They swore—and the answering sunlight
  Leaped red from their lifted swords,
And the hate in their hearts made echo
  To the wrath in their burning words.

There's weeping in all New England,
  And by Schuylkill's banks a knell,
And the widows there and the orphans,
  How the oath was kept, can tell.*

---

* It may add something to the interest with which these stirring lines will be read, to know that they were composed

SOUTHERN MARSEILLAISE.

YE men of Southern hearts and feeling,
    Arm, Arm! your struggling country calls—
Hear ye the guns now loudly pealing,
    From Sumter's high embattled walls!
Shall a fanatic horde in power
    Send forth a base and hireling band,
    To desolate our happy land,
And make our Southern freemen cower.
        To arms, to arms! each one,
        The sword unsheathe, raise the gun,
        Then on, rush on, ye brave and free,
        To death or victory.

Now clouds of war begin to gather,
    And black and murky is our sky—
Shall we submit—no, never, never!
    Let death or freedom be our cry—
In Heaven's justice firm relying,
    We'll nobly struggle to be free,

---

within the walls of a Yankee Bastile. They reach us in manuscript, through the courtesy of a returned prisoner.—*Richmond Examiner.*

And bravely gain our liberty,
Or die, our Northern foes defying.
    To arms, to arms! each one, etc.

The peaceful homes of Texas burning,
  And Harper's Ferry's blood-stained soil,
Proclaim how strong their hearts are yearning
  For murder, pillage, crime, and spoil.
Shall we our feelings longer smother,
  And bear with patience yet our wrongs,
    Their jeers, their crimes, their taunts and thongs,
And greet them still as friend and brother?
    To arms, to arms! each one, etc.

Their tyranny we'll bear no longer,
  But burst asunder every tie,
Although in numbers they are stronger,
  We will be free, or we will die!
Too long the South has wept, bewailing
  That falsehood's dagger Yankees wield,
  But freedom is our sword and shield,
And all their arts are unavailing.
    To arms, to arms, each one, etc.

Beauregard Songster.

RICHMOND ON THE JAMES.

BY G. T. BURGESS.

A soldier of our army lay gasping on the field,
When battle's shock was over, and the foe was forced to yield.
He fell a youthful hero, before the foemen's aims,
On a blood-red field near Richmond, near Richmond on the James.

But one still stood beside him, his comrade in the fray,
They had been friends together through boyhood's happy day,
And side by side had struggled on field of blood and flames,
To part that eve near Richmond, near Richmond on the James.

He said, "I charge thee, comrade, the friend in days of yore,
Of the far, far distant dear ones that I shall see no more,

Though scarce my lips can whisper their dear and well-known names,
To bear to them my blessing from Richmond on the James.

"Bear my good sword to my brother, and the badge upon my breast,
To the young and gentle sister that I used to love the best;
But one lock from my forehead give my mother who still dreams
Of her soldier boy near Richmond—near Richmond on the James.

"Oh, I wish that mother's arms were folded round me now,
That her gentle hand could linger one moment on my brow,
But I know that she is praying where our blessed hearth-light gleams,
For her soldier's safe return from Richmond on the James.

"And on my heart, dear comrade, close lay those nut-brown braids,
Of one who was the fairest of all our village maids;

We were to have been wedded, but death the bridegroom claims,
And she is far, that loves me, from Richmond on the James.

"Oh, does the pale face haunt her, dear friend, that looks on thee?
Or is she laughing, singing in careless girlish glee?
It may be she is joyous, and loves but joyous themes,
Nor dreams her love lies bleeding near Richmond on the James.

"And though I know, dear comrade, thou'lt miss me for a while,
When their faces—all that loved thee—again on thee shall smile;
Again thou'lt be the foremost in all their youthful games,
But I shall lie near Richmond—near Richmond on the James."

And far from all that loved him, that youthful soldier sleeps,
Unknown among the thousands of those his country weeps;

But no higher heart nor braver, than his, at sun-
    set's beams,
Was laid that eve near Richmond—near Rich-
    mond on the James.

The land is filled with mourning, from hall and
    cot left lone,
We miss the well-known faces that used to greet
    our own;
And long poor wives and mothers shall weep,
    and titled dames,
To hear the name of Richmond—of Richmond
    on the James.

FROM THE SOUTH TO THE NORTH.

BY C. L. S.

THERE is no union when the hearts
    That once were bound together
Have felt the stroke that coldly parts
    All kindly ties forever.
Then oh! your cruel hands draw back,
    And let us be divided

In peace, since it is proved we lack
   The grace to live united.

We can not bear your scorn and pride,
   Your malice and your taunting,
That have for years our patience tried—
   Your hypocritic canting.
We WILL not bow our necks beneath
   The yoke that you decree us,
We WILL be free, though only death
   Should have the power to free us!

Oh, Southern sons are bold to dare,
   And Southern hearts courageous.
Nor meekly will they longer bear
   Oppression so outrageous.
And you shall feel our honest wrath,
   If hearts so cold *can* feel;
Shall meet us in your Southern path
   And prove our Southern steel.

We ask no favor at your hand,
   No gifts and no affection;
But only peace upon our land,
   And none of your protection.

We ask you now, henceforth, to know
   We are a separate nation;
And be assured we'll fully show
   We scorn your "proclamation."

We were not first to break the peace,
   That blessed our happy land;
We loved the quiet, calm, and ease,
   Too well to raise a hand,
Till fierce oppression stronger grew,
   And bitter were your sneers—
Then to our land we must be true,
   Or show a coward's fears!

We loved our banner while it waved
   An emblem of our Union,
The fiercest danger we had braved
   To guard that sweet communion.
But when it proved that "stripes" alone
   Were for our sunny South,
And all the "stars" in triumph shone
   Above the chilly North—

Then, not till then, our voices rose
   In one tumultuous wave—

We WILL the tyranny oppose,
  Or find a bloody grave!
Another flag shall lead our hosts
  To battle on the plain,
The "rebels" will defy your boasts,
  And prove your sneering vain!

There is no danger we could fear—
  No hardship or privation—
To free the land we hold so dear,
  From tyrannous dictation.
Blockade her ports—her seas shall swell
  Beneath your ships of war,
And every breeze in anger tell
  Your tyranny afar.

Her wealth may fail—her commerce droop
  With every foreign nation;
But mark you, if her pride shall stoop,
  Or her determination!
The products of her fields will be
  For food and raiment too—
From mountain cliff to rolling sea
  Her children will be true.

Her banner may not always wave
  On victory's fickle breath,
The young, chivalrous, and the brave,
  May feel the hand of death.
But, when her gallant sons have died,
  Her daughters will remain—
Nor crushed will be the Southern pride,
  Till they too, all are slain.

A BALLAD OF THE WAR.

BY GEORGE HERBERT SASS, OF S. C.

WATCHMAN, what of the night?
  Through the city's darkening street,
Silent and slow, the guardsmen go
  On their long and lonely beat.

Darkly, drearily down,
  Falleth the wintry rain;
And the cold gray mist hath the roof-tops kissed,
  As it glides o'er town and plain.

Beating against the windows,
  The sleet falls heavy and chill,
And the children draw nigher 'round hearth and
    fire,
  As the blast shrieks loud and shrill.

Silent is all without
  Save the sentry's challenge grim,
And a hush sinks down o'er the weary town
  And the sleeper's eyes are dim.

Watchman, what of the night?
  Hark! from the old church tower
Rings loud and clear, on the wintry air,
  The chime of the midnight hour.

But another sound breaks in,
  A summons deep and rude,
The roll of the drum, and the rush and hum
  Of a gathering multitude.

And the dim and flickering torch
  Sheds a red and lurid glare,
O'er the long dark line, where bayonets shine
  Faintly, yet sternly there.

A BALLAD OF THE WAR.

A low, deep voice is heard:
  "Rest on your arms, my men."
Then the muskets clank through each serried rank,
  And all is still again.

Pale faces and tearful eyes
  Gaze down on that grim array,
For a rumor hath spread that that column dread
  Marcheth ere break of day.

Marcheth against "the rebels,"
  Whose camp lies heavy and still,
Where the driving sleet and the cold rain beat
  On the brow of a distant hill.

And the mother's heart grows faint,
  As she thinks of her darling one,
Who perchance may lie 'neath that wintry sky,
  Ere the long, dark night be done.

Pallid and haggard, too,
  Is the cheek of the fair young wife;
And her eye grows dim as she thinks of him
  She loveth more than life.

For fathers, husbands, sons,
  Are the "rebels" the foe would smite,
And earnest the prayer for those lives so dear,
  And a bleeding country's right.

And where their treasure is,
  There is each loving heart;
And sadly they gaze by the torch's blaze,
  And the tears unbidden start.

Is there none to warn the camp,
  None from that anxious throng?
Ah, the rain beats down o'er plain and town—
  The way is dark and long.

No *man* is left behind,
  None that is brave and true,
And the bayonets bright, in the lurid light,
  With menace stern shine through.

Guarded is every street,
  Brutal the hireling foe;
Is there one heart here will boldly dare
  So brave a deed to do?

Look! in her still, dark room,
   Alone a woman kneels,
With Care's deep trace on her pale, worn face
   And Sorrow's ruthless seals.

Wrinkling her placid brow,
   A matron, she, and fair,
Though wan her cheek, and the silver streak
   Gemming her glossy hair.

A moment in silent prayer
   Her pale lips move, and then,
Through the dreary night, like an angel bright,
   On her mission of love to men.

She glideth upon her way,
   Through the lonely, misty street,
Shrinking with dread as she hears the tread
   Of the watchman on his beat.

Onward, ay, onward still,
   Far past the weary town,
Till languor doth seize on her feeble knees,
   And the heavy hands hang down.

But bravely she struggles on,
  Breasting the cold, dank rain,
And, heavy and chill, the mist from the hill
  Sweeps down upon the plain.

Hark! far behind she hears
  A dull and muffled tramp;
But before her the gleam of the watch-fire's beam
  Shines out from the Southern camp.

She hears the sentry's challenge,
  Her work of love is done;
She has fought a good fight, and on Fame's
      proud height
  Hath a crown of glory won.

Oh, they tell of a Tyrol maiden,
  Who saved from a ruthless foe
Her own fair town, 'mid its mountains brown,
  Three hundred years ago.

And I've read in tales heroic
  How a noble Scottish maid
Her own life gave, her king to save
  From foul assassin's blade.

But if these, on the rolls of honor,
  Shall live in lasting fame,
Oh, close beside, in grateful pride,
  We'll write this matron's name.

And when our fair-haired children
  Shall cluster round our knee,
With wondering gaze, as we tell of the days
  When we swore that we would be free,

We'll tell them the thrilling story,
  And we'll say to each childish heart,
"By this gallant deed, at thy country's need,
  Be ready to do thy part."

Southern Field and Fireside.

LAND OF THE SOUTH.

BY A. F. LEONARD.

Air—"*Friend of my Soul.*"

Land of the South! the fairest land
  Beneath Columbia's sky!
Proudly her hills of freedom stand,
  Her plains in beauty lie.

Her dotted fields, her traversed streams
   Their annual wealth renew.
Land of the South! in brightest dreams
   No dearer spot we view.

Men of the South! a free-born race,
   They vouch a patriot line;
Ready the foemen's van to face,
   And guard their country's shrine.
By sire and son a haloing light
   Through time is borne along—
They "nothing ask but what is right,
   And yield to nothing wrong."

Fair of the South! rare beauty's crown
   Ye wear with matchless grace;
No classic fair of old renown
   Deserve a higher place.
Your vestal robes alike become
   The palace and the cot;
Wives, mothers, daughters! every home
   Ye make a cherished spot.

Flag of the South! aye, fling its folds
   Upon the kindred breeze;
Emblem of dread to tyrant holds—
   Of freedom on the seas.

Forever may its stars and stripes
   In cloudless glory wave;
Red, white, and blue—eternal types
   Of nations free and brave!

States of the South! the patriot's boast!
   Here equal laws have sway;
Nor tyrant lord, nor despot host,
   Upon the weak may prey.
Then let them rule from sea to sea,
   And crown the queenly isle—
Union of love and liberty,
   'Neath Heaven's approving smile!

God of the South! protect this land
   From false and open foes!
Guided by Thine all-ruling hand,
   In vain will hate oppose.
So mote the ship of State move on
   Upon the unfathomed sea;
Gallantly o'er its surges borne,
   The bulwark of the free.

THERE'S LIFE IN THE OLD LAND YET!

BY JAS. R. RANDALL.

By blue Patapsco's billowy dash,
    The tyrant's war-shout comes,
Along with the cymbal's fitful clash,
    And the growl of his sullen drums.
We hear it! we heed it, with vengeful thrills,
    And we shall not forgive or forget;
There's faith in the streams, there's hope in the hills,
    There's life in the old land yet!

Minions! we sleep, but we are not dead;
    We are crushed, we are scourged, we are scarred;
We crouch—'tis to welcome the triumph tread
    Of the peerless BEAUREGARD.
Then woe to your vile, polluting horde,
    When the Southern braves are met;
There's faith in the victor's stainless sword,
    There's life in the old land yet!

Bigots! ye quell not the valiant mind,
    With the clank of an iron chain,

The spirit of freedom sings in the wind,
   O'er *Merryman, Thomas,* and *Kane;*
And we, though we smite not, are not thralls,
   Are piling a gory debt;
While down by McHenry's dungeon-walls
   There's life in the old land yet!

Our women have hung their harps away,
   And they scowl on your brutal bands,
While the nimble poignard dares the day,
   In their dear defiant hands.
They will strip their tresses to string our bows,
   Ere the Northern sun is set;
There's faith in their unrelenting woes,
   There's life in the old land yet!

There's life, though it throbbeth in silent veins,
   'Tis vocal without noise,
It gushed o'er Manassas's solemn plains,
   From the blood of the MARYLAND BOYS!
That blood shall cry aloud, and rise
   With an everlasting threat;
By the death of the brave, by the God in the skies.
   There's life in the old land yet!

THE MEN.

BY MAURICE BELL.

In the dusk of the forest shade
    A sallow and dusty group reclined;
Gallops a horseman up the glade—
    "Where will I your leader find?
Tidings I bring from the morning's scout—
    I've borne them o'er mound, and moor, and fen."
"Well, sir, stay not hereabout,
    Here are only a few of 'the men.'

"Here no collar has bar or star,
    No rich lacing adorns a sleeve;
Further on our officers are,
    Let them your news receive.
Higher up, on the hill up there,
    Overlooking this shady glen,
There are their quarters—don't stop here,
    We are only some of 'the men.'

"Yet stay, courier, if you bear
    Tidings that the fight is near,
Tell them we're ready, and that where
    They wish us to be we'll soon appear;

Tell them only to let us know
   Where to form our ranks, and when;
And we'll teach the vaunting foe
   That they've met a few of 'the men.'

"We're *the men*, though our clothes are worn—
   We're *the men*, though we wear no lace—
We're *the men*, who the foe have torn,
   And scattered their ranks in dire disgrace;
We're the men who have triumphed before—
   We're the men who will triumph again;
For the dust, and the smoke, and the cannon's roar,
   And the clashing bayonets—'*we're the men.*'

"Ye who sneer at the battle-scars,
   Of garments faded, and soiled and bare,
Yet who have for the 'stars and bars'
   Praise, and homage, and dainty fare;
Mock the wearers and pass them on,
   Refuse them kindly word, and then
Know, if your freedom is ever won
   By human agents—*these are the men!*"

THE CONFEDERATE FLAG.

BY J. R. BARRICK.

Flag of the South! Flag of the free!
  Thy stars shall cheer each eye,
Thy folds a sacred banner be,
  To all beneath our sky;
From where the blue Ohio flows,
  Far to the sea-gulf's stream,
Borne by each gentle breath that blows,
  Thy hues shall flush and gleam.

Flag of the South! Flag of the free!
  Type of a new estate,
Thy folds shall wave o'er land and sea,
  And heart and home elate;
At thy approach shall tyrants quail
  And despots, trembling, flee;
Nor wrong thy sway of right assail—
  Nought mar thy liberty.

Flag of the South! Flag of the free!
  Bright symbol of a land
Wrung from the grasp of tyranny,
  Ere fettered heart and hand;

Freedom fixed in thy firm embrace,
  A home for age shall find,
Linking the high hopes of our race
  With the grand march of mind.

Flag of the South! Flag of the free!
  The one to which we clung
In years agone, hath ceased to be
  The pride on which we hung;
Long trampled in the dust, that flag
  Hath lost the charm it bore;
No longer vale, and glen, and crag,
  Swell with its praise of yore.

Flag of the South! Flag of the free!
  Type of the Land of Flowers;
Thy stars shall light our victory
  O'er all contending powers;
Where law and order still shall reign,
  Thou shalt a signal be
To man, that he may still attain
  The boon of Liberty!

GLASGOW, KY.

"STONEWALL JACKSON'S WAY."

Come, stack arms, men! Pile on the rails,
  Stir up the camp-fire bright;
No matter if the canteen fails,
  We'll make a roaring night.
Here Shenandoah brawls along,
There burly Blue Ridge echoes strong,
To swell the brigade's rousing song
  Of " Stonewall Jackson's Way."

We see him now—the old slouched hat
  Cocked o'er his eye askew,
The shrewd, dry smile, the speech so pat,
  So calm, so blunt, so true.
The " Blue-Light Elder" knows 'em well;
Says he, " That's Banks—he's fond of shell;
Lord save his soul! we'll give him ——" well,
  That's " Stonewall Jackson's way."

Silence! ground arms! kneel all! caps off!
  Old Blue-Light's going to pray.
Strangle the fool that dares to scoff!
  Attention! it's his way.

Appealing from his native sod,
In forma pauperis to God—
"Lay bare thine arm, stretch forth thy rod!
   Amen!" That's "Stonewall's way."

He's in the saddle now. Fall in!
   Steady! the whole brigade!
Hill's at the ford, cut off—we'll win
   His way out, ball and blade!
What matter if our shoes are worn?
What matter if our feet are torn?
"Quick-step! we're with him before dawn!"
   That's "Stonewall Jackson's way."

The sun's bright lances rout the mists
   Of morning, and by George!
Here's Longstreet struggling in the lists,
   Hemmed in an ugly gorge.
Pope and his Yankees, whipped before;
"Bay'nets and grape!" hear Stonewall roar;
"Charge, Stuart! Pay off Ashby's score!"
   Is "Stonewall Jackson's way."

Ah, maiden! wait, and watch, and yearn
   For news of Stonewall's band!

Ah! widow, read with eyes that burn,
   That ring upon thy hand.
Ah! wife, sew on, pray on, hope on!
Thy life shall not be all forlorn.
The foe had better ne'er been born
   That gets in "Stonewall's way."

GONE TO THE BATTLE-FIELD.

BY JOHN ANTROBUR.

The reaper has left the field,
   The mower has left the plain;
And the reaper's hook, and the mower's scythe,
   Are changed to the sword again;
For the voice of a hundred years ago,
When Freedom struck her mightiest blow,
   Thrills every heart and brain.

The way-side mill is still,
   And the wheel drips all alone,
For the miller's brother, and son, and sire,
   And the miller's self have gone;

And their wives and daughters, tarrying still,
With smiles and tears about the mill,
   Wave, wave their heroes on.

The grain is full and ripe,
   And the harvest-moon is nigh,
But the farmer's son is among the slain,
   And the father heard the cry;
And his ancient eyes flashed fires of old,
His hoary head rose strong and bold,
   As, wild, he hurried by.

The corn is yet a-field,
   But many a stalk is red;
Yet not with the autumn-tassel stained,
   But the blood of heroes shed;
And their blood cries out from heaps of slain:
Oh, brothers, leave the sheaves of grain;
   On, to the fields of the dead!

By every quiet farm,
   Whence father and son had gone,
The fairest daughters of the land,
   Brave-hearted, cheer us on,
With the tender smiles that shelter tears,
And words to thrill a soldier's ears,
   When bloody fields are won.

Scarcely the form of man
   Was seen on the long highway ;
But patriot age, whose withered hands
   Stretched feebly up to pray,
And children whose voices haunt us still,
Gathered on every knoll and hill,
   Cheering us on our way.

Yonder, with feeble limbs,
   A matron, with silver hair,
Knelt, trembling, down on the soldier's path,
   And breathed to heaven a prayer,
With quivering lips, with streaming eyes:
"O God! preserve these gallant boys;
   In battle, be Thou there!"

O, soldiers! such as these
   Like household memories come ;
For a thousand prayers ascend to-day
   From those we left at home;
For the red, red field to-night may be
Our couch, our grave—while Victory
   Shall shout above our tomb.

In battle's bloody hour
   These pictures shall arise,

Of mothers, sisters, wives, and homes,
  And red and streaming eyes;
And every arm shall stronger be,
For home, for God, for liberty,
  And strike, while mercy dies.
      HEADQUARTERS, *9th Regt. Virginia Vols.*

RE-ENLISTMENT.

BY MRS. MARGARITA J. CANEDO.

WHAT! shall we now throw down the blade,
  And doff the helmet from our brows?
Now see our holy cause betrayed,
  And recreant prove to all our vows?
When first we drew these patriot swords,
  "A nation's freedom!" was the cry;
Our faith was pledged in these proud words,
  And heaven has sealed the oath on high.

Since then on dear-bought battle-plains
  We've seen our martyr brethren die,
While on the soil that drank those stains,
  Their native earth where now they lie,

The foe now treads—th' exulting foe,
    And desecrates the hero-graves.
Say, can we peace or honor know
    While there the accursèd banner waves?

Dear are our homes, that smile afar;
    Oft in the weary soldier's dreams,
While resting from the toils of war,
    He sees the light that round them beams.
Dear are the loved and lovely maids
    Shrined in the patriot soldier's heart;
Yet, while the foe our land invades,
    In vain the longing tear may start.

No! let the despot's hireling band,
    Who feel not honor—know not faith,
Who war not for their native land,
    Fly trembling from a dreaded death.
Our lives are to our country pledged,
    ·Until her last red field is won;
For "liberty or death" is waged
    The war where fights her faithful son.

Then plant that flag-staff in the earth,
    And round it rally, every son

Who loves the State that gave him birth,
  Till her proud sovereignty be won.
What though our limbs be weak with toil,
  What though we bear full many a scar;
Huzza! here's to our native soil,
  We re-enlist, and for the war!

SOUTHLAND.

THE PRIZE SONG.*

They sing of the East,
  With its flowery feast,
And clime of the North, with its mountains of snow;
  But give me the land
  Where the breezes blow bland,
O'er realms of magnolia and myrtle below.

---

* The publisher of "The Southern Soldier's Prize Songster," Mr. W. F. Wisely, of Mobile, Alabama, "determined to use his efforts to produce a collection of original songs, solely by Southern writers, "offered a premium of fifty dollars" for the best song suited to the present time. A committee of three gentlemen (Rev. Dr. Pierce, Hon. Percy Walker, and G. Y. Overall, Esq.) were appointed to make the award. Near thirty pieces were submitted in competition, most of them

The land of the South,
The fair sunny South,
The flower-crowned South,
In its *grandeur* for me.

Her sons are aye brave,
And no chains can enslave,
Though countless the hordes of their foemen may be;
Ah! see, even now,
As with battle-stained brow,
They vanquish the Northmen on land and on sea!
The land of the South,
The young gallant South,
The invincible South,
In its *valor* for me.

---

possessing high literary merit. After much deliberation, the committee selected the piece entitled "Southland," as the most meritorious. The author's name was not given, he only requesting in his note that the money, if awarded him, should be paid over for the benefit of our necessitous soldiers. This modesty will add to the attractiveness of his piece, which is the first in the present volume."—*Preface to "The Southern Soldier's Prize Songster, containing Martial and Patriotic Pieces (chiefly original) applicable to the present war. Mobile, Ala.: W. F. Wisely, No.* 38 *St. Michael St.,* 1864."

Her daughters are fair
As the pure lilies there,
And cheer her brave soldiers for freedom to die;
Their smiles are the light
Of the war-clouded night,
Their tears are sweet dew-drops distilled from the sky.
  The land of the South,
  The sweet rosy South,
  The starry-gemmed South,
  In its *beauty* for me!

In green blossomed dales,
And in violet vales,
And fields white with cotton, its dwellings once stood;
The spoilers now seek
Their vile vengeance to wreak,
And darken this Eden with ashes and blood!
  The land of the South,
  The opulent South,
  The long-plundered South,
  In its *richness* for me!

Oh, who would not stand
With his life in his hand,

To shield such a land from the feet of the foe?
  God made it thus free,
  And oh, perish must we,
Before it can be in bondage laid low!
  The land of the South,
  The proud sovereign South,
  The God-shielded South,
  In its *freedom* for me!

BEYOND THE POTOMAC.

BY PAUL H. HAYNE.*

They slept on the fields which their valor had won!
But arose with the first early blush of the sun,
For they knew that a great deed remained to be done,
  When they passed o'er the River.

---

* This piece was originally published in the "Richmond Whig" at the time of "Stonewall" Jackson's last descent upon Maryland.

They rose with the sun, and caught life from
    his light—
Those giants of courage, those Anaks in fight—
And they laughed out aloud in the joy of their
    might,
      Marching swift for the River.

On! on! like the rushing of storms through the
    hills—
On! on! with a tramp that is firm as their wills—
And the one heart of thousands grows buoyant
    and thrills,
      At the thought of the River.

On! the sheen of their swords! the fierce gleam
    of their eyes,
It seemed as on earth a new sunlight would rise,
And, king-like, flash up to the sun in the skies,
      O'er the path to the River.

But their banners, shot-scarred, and all darkened
    with gore,
On a strong wind of morning streamed wildly
    before,
Like the wings of Death-angels swept fast to the
    shore,
      The green shore of the River.

As they march—from the hill-side, the hamlet, the stream—
Gaunt throngs, whom the Foeman had manacled, teem,
Like men just roused from some terrible dream,
    To pass o'er the River.

They behold the broad banners, blood-darkened, yet fair,
And a moment dissolves the last spell of despair,
While a peal as of victory swells on the air,
    Rolling out to the River.

And that cry, with a thousand strange echoings spread,
Till the ashes of heroes seemed stirred in their bed,
And the deep voice of passion surged up from the dead—
    Ay! press on to the River.

On! on! like the rushing of storms through the hills,
On! on! with a tramp that is firm as their wills,
And the one heart of thousands grows buoyant, and thrills,
    As they pause by the River.

Then the wan face of Maryland, haggard and worn,
At that sight, lost the touch of its aspect forlorn,
And she turned on the Foeman full statured in scorn,
    Pointing stern to the River.

And Potomac flowed calm, scarcely heaving her breast,
With her low-lying billows all bright in the west,
For the hand of the Lord lulled the waters to rest
    Of the fair rolling River.

Passed! passed! the glad thousands march safe through the tide.
(Hark, Despot! and hear the wild knell of your pride,
Ringing weird-like and wild, pealing up from the side
    Of the calm flowing River.)

'Neath a blow swift and mighty the Tyrant shall fall,
Vain! vain! to his God swells a desolate call,
For his grave has been hollowed, and woven his pall,
    Since they passed o'er the River.

TRUE TO THE GRAY.

BY PEARL RIVERS.

I can not listen to your words, the land is long and wide ;
Go seek some happy Northern girl to be your loving bride ;
My brothers they were soldiers—the youngest of the three
Was slain while fighting by the side of gallant Fitzhugh Lee !

They left his body on the field (your side the day had won),
A soldier spurn'd him with his foot—*you* might have been the one ;
My lover was a soldier—he belonged to Gordon's band ;
A saber pierced his gallant heart—*yours* might have been the hand.

He reel'd and fell, but was not dead, a horseman spurred his steed,
And trampled on the dying brain—*you* may have done the deed :

I hold no hatred in my heart, no cold, unrighteous pride,
For many a gallant soldier fought upon the other side:

But still I can not kiss the hand that smote my country sore,
Nor love the foes who trampled down the colors that she bore;
Between my heart and yours there rolls a deep and crimson tide—
My brother's and my lover's blood forbid me be your bride.

The girls who loved the boys in gray—the girls to country true—
May ne'er in wedlock give their hands to those who wore the blue.

TELL THE BOYS THE WAR IS ENDED.

BY EMILY J. MOORE.

While in the first ward of the Quintard Hospital, Rome, Georgia, a young soldier, from the Eighth Arkansas Regiment, who had been wounded at Murfreesboro', called me to his bedside. As I approached I saw that he was dying, and when I bent over him he was just able to whisper, "Tell the boys the war is ended."

"Tell the boys the war is ended,"
   These were all the words he said;
"Tell the boys the war is ended,"
   In an instant more was dead.
Strangely bright, serene, and cheerful
   Was the smile upon his face,
While the pain, of late so fearful,
   Had not left the slightest trace.

"Tell the boys the war is ended,"
   And with heavenly visions bright
Thoughts of comrades loved were blended,
   As his spirit took its flight.
"Tell the boys the war is ended,"
   "Grant, O God, it may be so,"
Was the prayer which then ascended,
   In a whisper deep, though low.

"Tell the boys the war is ended,"
   And his warfare then was o'er,
As by angel bands attended,
   He departed from earth's shore.
Bursting shells and cannons roaring
   Could not rouse him by their din;
He to better worlds was soaring,
   Far from war, and pain, and sin.

BURN THE COTTON.

BY ESTELLE.

Burn the cotton! burn the cotton!
   Let the solemn triumph rise;
Fanned by Freedom's breath, its white wing
   Spreads her banner to the skies.
"Melt the bells" is but re-echoed
   O'er our valley's gathered pride,
Lay the cotton on the altar
   Where our loved have nobly died.

Burn the cotton! burn the cotton!
   Does this sacrifice compare

With the battle-field red flowing
  With the brave hearts offered there?
They no more shall strike for Freedom,
  Never worship at her shrine—
To hurl back the fell invader,
  To avenge them—it is thine.

Burn the cotton! burn the cotton!
  Down the Mississippi's tide
Let it thunder, till its valleys
  Catch the echo, far and wide—
Frowning in its wrath, it rises,
  Spreads its dark wing o'er the land,
Vetoes, in its swelling fury,
  Gain, to lure the robber band.

Burn the cotton! burn the cotton!
  Pile the white fleece high and higher,
Till the heavens reflect the glory
  Kindled by the patriot's fire.
This shall teach the haughty foeman,
  Startle him too late, to find
Chains were never made for freemen,
  Chains the Southern heart to bind.

Burn the cotton! burn the cotton!
  Flaming sparks, instead of seed,
Shall be sown in death and terror
  To the mongrel Yankee breed;
And the *crowns* who nod attendance
  On the treacherous Federal's lure,
Feel too late the want and ruin,
  Unjust favor can not cure.

Burn the cotton! burn the cotton!
  Let the record boldly stand;
Not a bale for " filthy lucre "—
  All for Freedom to our land.
Burn the cotton! burn the cotton!
  From its ashes there shall spring
Heralds of a new-born nation,
  Claiming still that "Cotton's King!"

MEMPHIS, TENN., *May* 16, 1862.

THE PRINTERS OF VIRGINIA TO "OLD ABE."

BY HARRY C. TREAKLE.

Though we're exempt, we're not the *metal*
   To keep in when duty calls;
But onward we will *press*, to settle
   This knotty *case*, with leaden *balls;*
For our dear old mother State, the *fount*
   From which we each our life did *take*,
Is *locked up* by a Vandal horde,
   And the honor of the *craft*'s at stake.

For *lean-faced* Lincoln's after us—
   His slim *shanks* moving like a scout;
But long before his *job* is done,
   He'll find that all his *quads* are *out*.
For with Lee our *headline*—worthy *guide*—
   We, *galley*-slaves will never be,
But still *press* onward by his side,
   For that *fat take*, sweet liberty!

Soon Abe will find what he's about
   Will cost him such a pile of rocks,
Before his cherished *work* is *out*,
   He'll have no *sorts* in any *box!*

For his *bank* is now so very low,
>   He scarce can *chase* up *quoins* to pay
The hired scum, the foreign foe,
>   Who comes to steal our rights away.

And his *chums* now see, by his *foul matter*,
>   To set *clean proof* he ne'er was *cast*,
And fears are felt that the gaunt old *ratter*
>   Will go *broadside* to *hell* at last,
Where his friend, the *devil*, will welcome him,
>   With *accents* sweet—to his bosom fly,
Revise his *foul proof-sheets* once more,
>   And *knock* his naked *form* in *pi*.

And so to rush the base old *monk* along,
>   And bring the quiet soon about,
We'll swell our *lines* to *columns* strong,
>   And give no quarters till he's *out;*
For Southern *jours.* now take a *stand*,
>   Their *foremen* marshaled at their *head*,
And each with *shooting-stick* in hand,
>   Resolved they will his *matter lead*.

And while a foe is in the field,
>   Our *hands* still steady, our *leaders* cool,
Death we'll *em-brace* before we'll yield ;
>   But, by God's help, we'll *stick* and *rule*,

And when, in after years to come,
  Our history's read by youth and sage,
They'll make a *side-note* of "well done,"
  On this our *volume's* brightest *page*.
NORFOLK, VA., *April* 4, 1862.

THE MARSEILLES HYMN.

Translated and adapted as an ode,

BY B. F. PORTER, OF ALABAMA.

SONS of the South, arise! awake! be free!
  Behold! the day of Southern glory comes.
See where the blood-stained flag of tyranny
  Pollutes the air that breathes around your homes.
Rise! Southern men, from villages and farms,
  Cry vengeance! Oh! shall worse than pirate slaves
Strangle your children in their mothers' arms,
  And spit on dust that fills your fathers' graves?
To arms! sons of the South! Come like a mountain-flood;
March on! let every vale o'erflow with the invaders' blood.

What would these men, whose lives black treachery stains—
  Conspirators, to plunder long endeared?
For whom these vile, these ignominious chains—
  These fetters, for our brother's hands prepared?
Sons of the South, for us! Oh! bitter thought!
  What transports should our burning souls inspire!
Shall Southern men, by mercenaries bought,
  Be sold to vassalage, from son to sire?
To arms! sons of the South! Come like a mountain-flood;
March on! let every vale o'erflow with the invaders' blood.

What! shall this groveling race, who cringe for gold,
  Make laws for Southern men, on Southern soil?
Shall these degenerate hordes, to avarice sold,
  Crush freedom's sons, and Freedom's altars spoil?
Great God! oh! by these iron-shackled hands,
  Ne'er shall our necks beneath their yokes be led.

Of despots such as these, shall Southern bands
  Ne'er own the mastery, till every heart is dead.
To arms! sons of the South! Come like a mountain-flood;
March on! let every vale o'erflow with the invaders' blood.

Tremble, O tyrants! and you, perfidious tools,
  Of every race and party long the scorn!
Tremble, ye base, ye parricidal fools,
  The doom of treachery is already born.
All Southern men are heroes in the fray;
  If fall they must, o'erpowered in the field,
Long as the race endures, each child for aye
  Shall from his cradle strike the sounding shield.
To arms! sons of the South! Come like a mountain-flood;
March on! let every vale o'erflow with the invaders' blood.

Sons of the South! magnanimous in war,
  Strike or withhold, as honor bids, your blows.
Spare, if you will, those victims from afar,
  Who, ignorant of liberty, become your foes.

But for these bastards of a free-born bed,
  These parasites, in Freedom's arms caressed,
These beasts, by sin and spoil and rapine bred,
  Who dig for blood, deep in their mother's breast,
To arms! sons of the South! Come like a mountain-flood;
March on! let every vale o'erflow with the invaders' blood.

O sacred love of country! For the South,
  Come, brave avengers, rush to every field.
Let cries of "Liberty" from every mouth
  Sound the alarm, till the base traitors yield.
Under our glorious flag, let Victory
  Respond to Freedom's call. Wipe off the stain
Of the invaders' feet. Dying, they will see
  Thy triumph, and the land redeemed again.
To arms! sons of the South! Come like a mountain-flood;
March on! let every vale o'erflow with the invaders' blood.

Nashville Gazette.

MONODY ON THE DEATH OF GENERAL STONEWALL JACKSON.

BY THE EXILE.

Aye, toll! toll! toll!
    Toll the funeral bell!
And let its mournful echoes roll
From sphere to sphere, from pole to pole,
O'er the flight of the greatest, kingliest soul
    That ever in battle fell.

Yes, weep! weep! weep!
    Weep for the hero fled!
For death, the greatest of soldiers, at last
Has over our leader his black pall cast,
And from us his noble form hath passed
    To the home of the mighty dead.

Then toll! and weep! and mourn!
    Mourn the fall of the brave!
For Jackson, whose deeds made the nation proud,
At whose very name the enemy cowed,
With the "crimson cross" for his martial shroud,
    Now sleeps his long sleep in the grave.

DEATH OF STONEWALL JACKSON.

His form has passed away;
    His voice is silent and still;
No more at the head of "the old brigade,"
The daring men who were never dismayed,
Will he lead them to glory that never can fade—
    Stonewall of the Iron Will!

He fell as a hero should fall;
    'Mid the thunder of war he died.
While the rifle cracked and the cannon roared,
And the blood of the friend and foeman poured,
He dropped from his nerveless grasp the sword
    That erst was the nation's pride.

Virginia, his mother, is bowed;
    Her tread is heavy and slow.
From all the South comes a wailing moan,
And mountains and valleys re-echo the groan,
For the gallant chief of her clans has flown,
    And a nation is filled with woe.

Rest, warrior! rest!
    Rest in thy laureled tomb!
Thy mem'ry shall live through all of earth's years,
And thy name still excite the despot's fears,
While o'er thee shall fall a nation's tears;
    Thy deeds shall not perish in gloom.

THE CONFEDERATE FLAG.

BY MRS. C. D. ELDER.

Bright banner of freedom, with pride I unfold
    thee;
Fair flag of my country, with love I behold thee,
Gleaming above us, in freshness and youth,
Emblem of liberty—symbol of truth;
For this flag of my country in triumph shall wave
O'er the Southerner's home and the Southerner's
    grave.

All bright are the stars that are beaming upon us,
And bold are the bars that are gleaming above
    us;
The one shall increase in their number and light,
The other grow bolder in power and might;
For this flag of my country in triumph shall wave
O'er the Southerner's home or the Southerner's
    grave.

Those bars of bright red show our firm resolution
To die, if need be, shielding thee from pollution;
For man in this hour must give all he holds
    dear,

And woman her prayers and her words of high
    cheer,
If they wish this fair banner in triumph to wave
O'er the Southerner's home and the Southerner's
    grave.

To the great God of battles we look with reliance;
On our fierce Northern foe with contempt and
    defiance;
For the South shall smile on in her fragrance and
    bloom
When the North is fast sinking in silence and
    gloom;
For the flag of our country in triumph must wave
O'er the Southerner's home or the Southerner's
    grave.

    NEW ORLEANS, LA.

THE SOUTH.

BY CHARLIE WILDWOOD.

THE bright rose of beauty, unnurtured by art,
And purity's lily doth thrive in thy heart,

While honor hath crowned thee with glory's bright
    ray,
And Flora hath decked thee with flowers of May.
Oh, beautiful South! cherished home of my birth,
Thou fairest, thou loveliest land of the earth!
My heart, like the ivy, still clings unto thee,
Oh, beautiful, beautiful land of the free!
    Chorus—The South! the South! my own beau-
        tiful South!
    Land of chivalry! home of liberty!
    Fondly I love thee, dear land of the
        South!
    Dear land of the South! dear land of
        the South!

Dear liberty, virtue, and truth, most sublime,
The flowers that bloom in that sun-smiling clime,
And these the base tyrant would crush to the
    earth,
And mangle and bruise on the soil of their birth.
All crimson thy land, with the life-glowing flood,
And dabble his hands in thy heart's reeking
    blood!
But oh! by the God of the righteous and free,
Bright region! it never! no, never! shall be.

Like swarms of foul demons, his minions come down,
And their war-rusted weapons insultingly frown,
To fright thy fair fields with their bloody alarms,
And rob thee, dear land, of all of thy charms.
But thy free spirit still rides on the swift gale,
Like the eagle that sweeps o'er the mountain and dale;
And thy sons, they rush forth with the courage of men,
To fight, and to bleed, and to conquer again.

The tyrant, with shackles, would manacle thee—
Would strangle thy spirit, dear land of the free,
Would trample the banner of right in the dust,
And yoke thee with iron, proud queen of the just!
But the hearts of thy sons, unappalled by a fear,
As their swords leap up fiercely and flame in the air,
Now swear that it never! no! never! shall be,
Bright queen of the lovely! sweet home of the free!

Chorus—The South! the South, etc.

THE GIRLS OF THE MONUMENTAL CITY.

WRITTEN BY A CONFEDERATE PRISONER.

Daughters of the sunny South,
  Where Freedom loves to dwell,
How rare your charms, how sweet your smiles,
  No mortal lips can tell;
Your native hills, the rippling rills,
  The echo wild and free,
Declare you born to hate and scorn
  All Northern tyranny.

Girls whose smiles are all reserved,
  The Southern youth to bless;
Whose hearts are kept for those who fight
  For Freedom's happiness;
Your spirits bold, so now unfold
  What willingly you would do,
Where Yankee spirit—the tyrants might
  Not wield against you.

For you your loving brothers rush
  To overthrow the invader's might—
On martial field the sword they wield,
  And Yankee cowards smite.

May heaven bless, with bright success,
    Each glorious Southern son;
Be this your prayer, O maidens fair!
    And our freedom will be won.

Southern girls, on this we've sworn,
    The South *must—shall be free—*
No Northern shackles will be worn;
    To them we'll bend no knee.
From hill to hill, exultant, shrill,
    Our battle-cry rings forth:
Freedom or death on every breath,
    And hatred to the North.

Cease not to smile, brave Southern girls,
    On our efforts to be free—
Whilst life remains, we'll struggle on,
    Till all the world shall see
That those who fight for home and right
    Can never be enslaved;
Their blood may stain the battle-plain;
    Our country must be saved.

BALTIMORE, MD., *March*, 1862.

WAR SONG OF THE PARTISAN RANGERS.

BY BENJAMIN F. PORTER.

Air—*McGregor's Gathering.*

The forests are green by the homes of the South,
But the hearth-stones are red with the blood of
    her youth;
Unfurl the black banner o'er mountain and vale,
Let the war-cry of vengeance swell loud on the
    gale.
  Then gather, gather, gather, gather, gather;
  While there's leaf in the forest, and foam on
    the river,
  The cry of the South shall be Vengeance
    Forever!

Each drop of the blood of our children they've
    shed,
Our foes shall atone for, in heaps of their dead;
The signal for fight which our forefathers knew,
Shall be heard in their midst in our vengeful
    halloo.
  Then gather, gather, etc.

WAR SONG OF THE PARTISAN RANGERS.

Thro' their cities our horsemen, with sword and with flame,
Shall carry the dread of the Southerner's name!
At the sound of our bugles their strong men shall quail,
And the cheeks of their wives and their mothers turn pale.
    Then gather, gather, etc.

They have blasted our fields, they have slaughtered our youth,
And dishonored the names of the maids of the South;
But the rivers shall dry, and the mountains be riven,
Ere vengeance be quenched or our wrongs be forgiven.
    Then gather, gather, etc.

Then rally from forest and rally from ford,
Give their homes to the flames, and their sons to the sword;
While a child shall be born in the South, let its cry
Be, "Death to the Northmen, and vengeance for aye!"

Greenville, Ala., Observer.

THE BAND IN THE PINES.

BY JOHN ESTEN COOKE.*

OH, band in the pine-wood, cease!
   Cease with your splendid call;
The living are brave and noble,
   But the dead were bravest of all!

They throng to the martial summons,
   To the loud, triumphant strain;
And the dear bright eyes of long-dead friends
   Come to the heart again!

They come with the ringing bugle,
   And the deep drum's mellow roar;
Till the soul is faint with longing
   For the hands we clasp no more!

Oh, band in the pine-woods, cease!
   Or the heart will melt in tears,
For the gallant eyes and the smiling lips,
   And the voices of old years.

---

* Heard after Pelham died.

SONG OF OUR GLORIOUS SOUTHLAND.

BY MRS. MARY WARE.

I.

Oh, sing of our glorious Southland,
   The pride of the golden sun!
'Tis the fairest land of flowers
   The eye e'er looked upon.

Sing of her orange and myrtle,
   That glitter like gems above;
Sing of her dark-eyed maidens
   As fair as a dream of love.

Sing of her flowing rivers—
   How musical their sound!
Sing of her dark-green forests,
   The Indian hunting-ground.

Sing of the noble nation,
   Fierce struggling to be free;
Sing of the brave who barter
   Their lives for liberty!

II.

Weep for the maid and matron
  Who mourn their loved ones slain;
Sigh for the light departed,
  Never to shine again.

'Tis the voice of Rachel weeping,
  That never will comfort know;
'Tis the wail of desolation,
  The breaking of hearts in woe!

III.

Ah! the blood of Abel crieth
  For vengeance from the sod!
'Tis a brother's hand that's lifted
  In the face of an angry God!

Oh! brother of the Northland,
  We plead from our father's grave;
We strike for our homes and altars,
  He fought to build and save!

A smoldering fire is burning,
  The Southern heart is steeled—
Perhaps 'twill break in dying,
  But never will it yield.

OLD BETSY.

BY JOHN KILLUM.

Come, with the rifle so long in your keeping,
    Clean the old gun up and hurry it forth;
Better to die while "Old Betsy" is speaking
    Than live with arms folded the slave of the North.

Hear ye the yelp of the North-wolf resounding,
    Scenting the blood of the warm-hearted South;
Quick! or his villainous feet will be bounding
    Where the gore of our maidens may drip from his mouth.

Oft in the wildwood "Old Bess" has relieved you,
    When the fierce bear was cut down in his track—
If at that moment she never deceived you,
    Trust her to-day with this ravenous pack.

Then come, with the rifle so long in your keeping,
    Clean the old girl up and hurry her forth;

Better to die while "Old Betsy" is speaking
 Than live with arms folded the slave of the North.

NO SURRENDER.

EVER constant, ever true,
 Let the word be, No Surrender.
Boldly dare and greatly do!
They shall bring us safely through,
 No Surrender; No Surrender.
And though Fortune's smiles be few,
Hope is always springing new,
Still inspiring me and you,
 With a magic No Surrender.

Nail the colors to the mast,
 Shouting gladly, No Surrender;
Troubles near are all but past,
Serve them as you did the last.
 No Surrender, No Surrender;
Though the skies be overcast,
And upon the sleety blast
Disappointment gathers fast,
 Beat them off with No Surrender!

Constant and courageous still,
  Mind, the word is, No Surrender;
Battle, though it be up hill,
Stagger not at seeming ill,
  No Surrender, No Surrender.
Hope, and thus your hope fulfill;
There's a way where there's a will,
And the way all cares to kill
  Is to give them No Surrender.

N. P. W.

ARM FOR THE SOUTHERN LAND.

BY GEN. MIRABEAU B. LAMAR.

ARM for the Southern Land,
  All fear of death disdaining;
Low lay the tyrant band,
  Our sacred rights profaning!
Each hero draws in Freedom's cause,
  And meets the foe with bravery;
The servile race, and Tory base,
  May safety seek in slavery.
Chains for the dastard knave—
  Recreant limbs should wear them;

But blessings on the brave
  Whose valor will not bear them!

Stand by your injured State,
  And let no feuds divide you;
On tyrants pour your hate,
  And common vengeance guide you.
Our foes should feel proud freemen's steel,
  For freemen's rights contending;
Where'er they die, there let them lie,
  To dust in scorn descending.
Thus may each traitor fall
  Who dare as foe invade us;
Eternal fame to all
  Who shall in battle aid us!

Proud land! shall she invoke
  Another's hand to right her?
No! her own avenging stroke
  Shall backward roll the smiter.
Ye tyrant band, with ropes of sand
  Go bind the rushing river;
More weak and vain your cursèd chain,
  While God is freedom's giver.
Then welcome to the day
  We meet the proud oppressor,

For God will be our stay,
  Our right hand and redresser.

THINKING OF THE SOLDIERS.

We were sitting around the table,
  Just a night or two ago,
In the little cozy parlor,
  With the lamp-light burning low,
And the window-blinds half opened,
  For the summer air to come,
And the painted curtains moving
  Like a busy pendulum.

Oh! the cushions on the sofa,
  And the pictures on the wall,
And the gathering of comforts,
  In the old familiar hall;
And the wagging of the pointer,
  Lounging idly by the door,
And the flitting of the shadows
  From the ceiling to the floor.

Oh! they wakened in my spirit,
  Like the beautiful in art,

Such a busy, busy thinking—
  Such a dreaminess of heart,
That I sat among the shadows,
  With my spirit all astray;
Thinking only—thinking only
  Of the soldiers far away;

Of the tents beneath the moonlight,
  Of the stirring tattoo's sound,
Of the soldier in his blanket,
  In his blanket on the ground;
Of the icy winter coming,
  Of the cold bleak winds that blow,
And the soldier in his blanket,
  In his blanket on the snow.

Of the blight upon the heather,
  And the frost upon the hill,
And the whistling, whistling ever,
  And the never, never still;
Of the little leaflets falling,
  With the sweetest, saddest sound—
And the soldier—oh! the soldier,
  In his blanket on the ground.

Thus I lingered in my dreaming,
  In my dreaming far away,
Till the spirit's picture-painting
  Seemed as vivid as the day;
And the moonlight faded softly
  From the window opened wide,
And the faithful, faithful pointer
  Nestled closer by my side.

And I knew that 'neath the starlight,
  Though the chilly frosts may fall,
That the soldier will be dreaming,
  Dreaming often of us all.
So I gave my spirit's painting
  Just the breathing of a sound,
For the dreaming, dreaming soldier,
  In his slumber on the ground.

November 24, 1861.

THE DYING SOLDIER.

BY JAMES A. MECKLIN.

GATHER round him where he's lying,
  Hush your footsteps, whisper low,

For a soldier here is dying,
   In the sunset's radiant glow.

Beating, beating, slowly beating,
   Runs the life-blood through his frame;
Swift the soldier's breath is fleeting,
   And he calls his mother's name:

"Mother, mother, come and kiss me,
   Ere my spirit fades away,
For I know you oft will miss me,
   When you watch the sinking day.

"Brother, sister, nearer, nearer!
   Place, oh, place your hands in mine,
You whose love than life was dearer,
   Let your arms around me twine.

"Father, see the sun is fading
   From the hill-tops of the west,
And the valley night is shading—
   Farewell, loved ones, I'm at rest."

Dying, dying! yes, he's dying!
   Close the eyelids, let him rest;
No more sorrow, no more sighing,
   E'er again shall heave his breast.

Sleeping, sleeping, calmly sleeping,
  In the church-yard cold and drear,
And the wintry winds are heaping
  O'er him leaflets brown and sear.

And he's resting, where forever
  Clang of trumpet, roll of drum,
Roar of cannon, never, never,
  Never more to him shall come.

PENSACOLA: TO MY SON.

BY M. S.

BEAUTIFUL the land may be,
  Its groves of palm, its laurel-trees,
And o'er the smiling, murm'ring sea,
  Soft may blow the Southern breeze—
And land, and sea, and balmy air,
May make a home of beauty there.

And bright beneath Floridian sky,
  The world to thy young fancy seems;
I see the light that fills thine eye,
  I know what spirit rules thy dreams;

But flower-gemmed shore and rippling sea
Are darker than the grave to me;

For storms are lowering in that sky,
  And sad may be that fair land's doom;
Full soon, perhaps, the battle-cry
  May wake the cannon's fearful boom,
And shot and shell from o'er the waves
May plow the rose's bed for graves.

And we, whose dear ones cluster there,
  We, mothers, who have let them go—
Our all, perhaps—how shall we bear
  That which another week may show?
The love which made our lives, all gone,
Our hearts left desolate and lone!

Country! what to *me* that name,
  Should I in vain demand my son?
Glory! what a nation's fame?
  Home! home, without thee, I have none;
Ah! stay—this Southern land not *mine?*
The land that e'en in death is thine!

A country's laurel-wreath for thee,
  A *hero's grave*—my own! my own!

And neither land nor home for *me*,
   Because a *mother's* hope is gone?
Traitor I am! God's laws command
That, NEXT TO HEAVEN, OUR NATIVE LAND!

And I will not retract—ah! no—
   What, in my pride of home, I said,
That, "*I would give my son to go
   Where'er our* HERO RULER *led!*"
The mother's heart may burst—but still,
Make it, O God, to know Thy will.
   NEW ORLEANS, LA.

THE VOLUNTEERS TO THE "MELISH."

BY WM. C. ESTRES.

COME forth, ye gallant heroes,
   Rub up each rusty gun,
And face these hireling Yankees,
   Who live by tap of drum.
We Volunteers are wearied,
   By a twelve months' "sojourn";
We want to rest a little,
   And then we'll fight "again."

We've won some five pitched battles,
   But will yield you our "posish";
And if you want some glory,
   Why pitch in now, "Melish."
Don't refuse to leave your spouses;
   Our own are just as dear,
And each lonely little woman
   Longs for her Volunteer.

Don't mind your sobbing sweethearts;
   For though 'tis hard to part,
We'll volunteer to cheer 'em,
   And console each troubled heart.
For the sake of old Virginia,
   Come and fight! *that's if you can,*
And let your prattling babies
   Know their daddy was a man.

For you *we've* fought and struggled;
   Had "no furloughs"—nary one—
We want a little resting,
   And so we're coming home.
Then *forward*, bold Militia!
   "If you're coming, come along,"
Or, by the gods! we'll force you out
   To your duty—right or wrong.

THE TURTLE.

Cæsar, afloat with his fortunes!
  And all the world agog,
Straining its eyes
At a thing that lies
  In the water, like a log!
It's a weasel! a whale!
I see its tail!
  It's a porpoise! a polywog!

Tarnation! it's a *turtle!*
  And blast my bones and skin,
My hearties, sink her,
Or else you'll think her
  A regular terror—pin!

The frigate poured a broadside!
  The bombs they whistled well,
But—hit old Nick
With a sugar stick!
  It didn't phase her shell!

Piff, from the creature's larboard—
  And dipping along the water

A bullet hissed
From a wreath of mist
  Into a Doodle's quarter!

Raff, from the creature's starboard—
  Rip, from his ugly snorter,
And the Congress and
The Cumberland
  Sunk, and nothing—shorter.

Now, here's to you, Virginia,
  And you are bound to win!
By your rate of bobbing round
  And your way of pitchin' in—
For you are a cross
Of the old sea-horse
  And a regular terror—pin.

JACKSON.

BY HENRY L. FLASH.

Not 'midst the lightning of the stormy fight,
  Not in the rush upon the vandal foe,
Did kingly Death, with his resistless might,
  Lay the Great Leader low.

His warrior soul its earthly shackles broke,
  In the full sunshine of a peaceful town;
When all the storm was hushed, the trusty oak
    That propped our cause, went down.

Though his alone the blood that flecks the ground,
  Recording all his grand, heroic deeds,
Freedom herself is writhing with the wound,
    And all the country bleeds.

He entered not the Nation's Promised Land
  At the red belching of the cannon's mouth;
But broke the House of Bondage with his hand—
    The Moses of the South!

O gracious God! not gainless is the loss:
  A glorious sunbeam gilds thy sternest frown;
And while his country staggers with the cross,
    He rises with the crown!

SONG OF THE PRIVATEER.

BY ALEX. H. CUMMINS.

FEARLESSLY the seas we roam,
  Tossed by each briny wave;
Its boundless surface is our home,
  Its bosom deep our grave.
No foreign mandate fills with awe
  Our gallant-hearted band;
We know no home, we know no law,
  But that of Dixie's land.

The bright star is our compass true,
  Our chart the ocean wide;
Our only hope the noble few
  That's standing side by side.
We do not fear the stormy gale
  That sweeps old ocean's strand;
We scorn our enemy's clumsy sail,
  And all for Dixie's land.

We love to hoist to the topmost peak
  Our Southern Stars and Stripes;
And woe to him who dares to seek
  To trample on their rights!

It is the ægis of the free,
  And by it we will stand,
And watch it waving o'er the sea,
  And over Dixie's land.

We love to roam the deep, deep sea,
  And hear the cannon's boom,
And give the war-cry wild and free
  Amid the battle's gloom.
We do not fight alone for gain,
  So far from native strand;
But our country's freedom and its fame,
  And the fair of Dixie's land.

NO UNION MEN.

BY MILLIE MAYFIELD.

"On the 21st, five of the enemy's steamers approached Washington, N. C., and landed a hundred Yankees, who marched through the town, playing 'Yankee Doodle,' hoisted their flag on the court-house, and destroyed gun-carriages and an unfinished gun-boat in the ship-yard. The people preserved a sullen and unresisting silence. The Yankees then left, saying they were disappointed in not finding Union men."—*Telegram from Charleston, March* 29, 1862.

"Union men!" O thrice-fooled fools!
   As well might ye hope to bind
The desert sands with a silken thread,
   When tossed by the whistling wind,
Or to blend the shattered waves that lash
   The feet of the cleaving rock,
When the tempest walks the face of the deep,
   And the water-spirits mock,
As the severed chain to reunite
   In a peaceful link again;
On our burning homesteads ye may write,
   "We found no Union men."

Aye, hoist your old dishonored flag,
   And pipe your worn-out tune;
The hills of the South have caught the strain,
   And will answer it full soon;
Not with the sycophantic tone,
   And the cringing knee bent low—
The deep-mouthed cannon shall bear the tale,
   Where the sword deals blow for blow;

Our braying trumpets in your ears,
   Shall defiant shout again,
"Back, wolves and foxes, to your lairs,
   Here are no Union men!"

Union, with tastes dissimilar?
   Such Union is the worst
And direst form of bondage that
   Nations or men have cursed!
Union with traitors? Hear ye not
   That cry for vengeance, deep,
Where hand to hand, and foot to foot,
   Our glittering columns sweep?
Our iron-tongued artillery
   Shouts through the bristling glen,
To the war-drum echoing reveillé,
   "Here are no Union men!"

Oh, deep have sunken the burning seeds
   That the wingèd winds have borne,
That for all your future years must yield
   The thistle and prison-thorn;
Our soil was genial—ye might have sown
   A harvest rich. 'Tis too late!
To our children's children we leave for you
   But a heritage of Hate!

Ye have opened the wild flood-gates of war,
    And we may not the torrent pen;
But ye seek in vain on our storm-beat shore
    For the myth called "Union Men."

HARP OF THE SOUTH.

A SONNET. BY "CORA."

Harp of the South, awake! A loftier strain
Than ever yet thy tuneful strings has stirred,
Awaits thee now. The Eastern world has heard
The thunder of the battle 'cross the main—
Has seen the young South burst the tyrant's chain,
And rise to being at a single word—
The watchword, Liberty—so long transferred
To the oppressor's mouth. Moons wax and wane,
And still the nations stand with listening ear,
And still o'er ocean floats the battle-cry.
Harp of the South, awake, and bid them hear
The name of Jackson; loud, and clear, and high,
Strike notes exultant, o'er the hero's bier,
Who, though he sleeps in dust, can never die.

WHAT THE SPIRITS OF THE FATHERS OF THE FIRST REVOLUTION SAY TO THEIR SONS NOW ENGAGED IN THE SECOND.

BY HENRY LOMAS.

WE are watching that land where Liberty woke—
Like beams of the morning through darkness it broke—
Then up from the mountain the bold eagle sprung,
And wide to the breeze his broad pinions flung.
    Rise! rise! ye sons of the South and be free!

The mighty have fallen, yet death can not chill,
Those noble emotions the soul ever thrill;
The grave hath no confines the spirit to hold,
While back to its kindred it flies to unfold
    Truth! Truth! safeguard of the South and the free.

Shall Washington rest, while a wail of discord
Reminds him the North is forgetting the Lord?

Will hero and statesman—the country's bright light—
Look down without pity from yonder far height,
   On this Land of Hope, for the brave and the free?

That same noble spirit now watches above,
With thousands of others, to guide and guard you with love;
For here, true, earnest, and brave men are found,
With hearts uncorrupted, to their native land bound.
   Awake! awake! O ye sons of the South, and be free!

Down with the hireling that seeks now to rend
The homes which your ancestors fought to defend;
Rekindle the beacon ere the last spark is fled,
And light up the camp-fires round Liberty's bed!
   Ye sons of the sunny South, strike to be free!

Fear not the Northern despot, or his feeble frown,
Who seeks, through his minions, the South to put down;

Look to your God, from whence comes all power,
And seek His aid and protection in each darkened hour.
    Strike again and again, O ye sons of the free!

Carolina's sons to this platform have come—
Protection to Liberty, to fireside, and home—
Their watch-word to-day, as their Fathers' of old,
Truth, Justice, and Freedom, before Northern gold.
    Ye are the sons of the Fathers who bled to be free!

Then loud ring the anvil, the hammer, and bell;
The South her new anthem, say what does it tell?
Cotton, Grain, and Sugar, have proved threefold cord—
Columbia, the envied, the blest of the Lord!
    Sun of the sunny land, shine still o'er the free!

On heaven's fair arches, see graven the names
Of patriot and soldier, who drained life's pure veins;

Then down with the Northern despot, let him hide his head,
Who by heartless oppression would sever one thread
   Of this Southern Confederacy, the hope of the free!

Once again at the altar, brothers, gather and kneel;
Our pledge, the South—one family, in woe or in weal;
One God and one Country—in peace or in war;
The South, Free, United, and Truth the pole-star
   Of this sunny land, which for ye must be free!

HEART-VICTORIES.

BY A SOLDIER'S WIFE.

There's not a stately hall,
  There's not a cottage fair,
That proudly stands on Southern soil,
  Or softly nestles there,

But in its peaceful walls,
   With wealth or comfort blest,
A stormy battle fierce hath raged
   In gentle woman's breast.

There Love, the true, the brave,
   The beautiful, the strong,
Wrestles with Duty, gaunt and stern,
   Wrestles and struggles long;
He falls—no more again
   His giant foe to meet;
Bleeding at every opening vein,
   Love falls at Duty's feet.

Oh! daughter of the South!
   No victor's crown be thine;
Not thine, upon the tented field,
   In martial pomp to shine;
But, with unfaltering trust
   In Him who rules on high,
To deck thy loved ones for the fray,
   And send them forth to die.

With wildly throbbing heart—
   With faint and trembling breath—
The maiden speeds her lover on,
   To victory or death;

Forth from caressing arms,
   The mother sends her son,
And bids him nobly battle on,
   Till the last field is won.

While she, the tried, the true,
   The loving wife of years,
Chokes down the rising agony,
   Drives back the starting tears:
"I yield thee up," she cries,
   "In the country's cause to fight;
Strike for our own, our children's home,
   And God defend the right."

Oh! daughter of the South,
   When our fair land is free,
When peace her lovely mantle throws
   Softly o'er land and sea,
History shall tell, how thou
   Hast nobly borne thy part,
And won the proudest triumphs yet—
   The victories of the heart.

SEVENTY-SIX AND SIXTY-ONE.

BY JOHN W. OVERALL.

Ye spirits of the glorious dead!
    Ye watchers in the sky!
Who sought the patriot's crimson bed,
    With holy trust and high—
Come, lend your inspiration now,
    Come, fire each Southern son,
Who nobly fights for freemen's rights,
    And shouts for sixty-one.

Come, teach them how on hill, on glade,
    Quick leaping from your side,
The lightning flash of sabers made
    A red and flowing tide;
How well ye fought, how bravely fell,
    Beneath our burning sun,
And let the lyre, in strains of fire,
    So speak of sixty-one.

There's many a grave in all the land,
    And many a crucifix,
Which tells how that heroic band
    Stood firm in seventy-six—

Ye heroes of the deathless past,
   Your glorious race is run,
But from your dust springs freemen's trust,
   And blows for sixty-one.

We build our altars where you lie,
   On many a verdant sod,
With sabers pointing to the sky,
   And sanctified of God;
The smoke shall rise from every pile,
   Till Freedom's cause is won,
And every mouth throughout the South
   Shall shout for sixty-one!

KENTUCKY.

BY ESTELLE.

"Just send for us Kentucky boys,
   And we'll protect you, ladies."—*Old Song.*

THEN, leave us not, Kentucky boys,
   Though thick upon thy border,
The vulture flaps his restless wing,
   And scowls the dark marauder.

Kentucky blood is just as proud,
   Kentucky powder ready,
Kentucky hearts are just as brave,
   Kentucky nerve as steady,

As when the flag we once revered,
   Unfolded o'er her proudly,
And for the South, Kentucky's voice,
   Undaunted, echoed loudly.

The lion-hearted hero then,
   Who led that gallant number,
Must surely feel a sad unrest
   Disturb his death-cold slumber.

And one whose sire, on history's page,
   Is blent in proudest story,
Fell on a Southern field, and bathed
   His dying brow in glory.

Fell, overcome by savage foes,
   Yet still their rage defying;
"*These*, give my father," cried the son,
   "And tell him how I'm dying."

But now that flag is vilely stained,
  Its sacred rights invaded—
Wrong and dishonor wield the staff;
  Its glory's sadly shaded.

And when we would its dying spark
  Snatch from the blackening ashes,
And worship once again its light,
  As through the world it flashes,

Kentucky leans upon her arms,
  And coldly looks about her,
Till hirelings, at her very door,
  Dare threaten, and to flout her.

Desert us now, Kentucky boys,
  And on the future dawning,
Thy faded glory scarce will streak
  The first gray light of morning.

Heed not the starveling crew, who hang
  Upon the blue Ohio,
A craven heart each traitor bears,
  And dare not venture nigher.

And should they—know ye not the blood
　　Within our full hearts beaming?—
At once ten thousand scabbards fly,
　　Ten thousand blades are gleaming!

Then, waken from thy nerveless sleep,
　　Gird on thy well-tried armor,
And soon the braggart North will feel
　　That Right has strength to harm her.

Kentucky boys and girls have we—
　　From us ye may not take them;
Sad-hearted will ye give them up,
　　And for the foe forsake them?

Oh, Tennessee, twin-sister, grieves,
　　To take thy hand at parting,
And feel that from its farewell grasp
　　A brother's blood is starting.

It must not be! Kentucky, come!
　　Virginia loudly calls thee;
And Maryland defenseless stands,
　　To share what fate befalls thee.

Come ere the tyrant's chain is forged,
  From out the war-cloud looming;
Come ere thy palsied knee is bent,
  To hopeless ruin dooming.

A POEM WHICH NEEDS NO DEDICATION.

BY JAMES BARRON HOPE.

What! you hold yourselves as freemen?
  Tyrants love just such as ye!
Go! abate your lofty manner!
Write upon the State's old banner,
  "A furore Normanorum,
  Libera nos, O Domine!"

Sink before the Federal altars,
  Each one, low on bended knee;
Pray, with lips that sob and falter,
This prayer from a coward's Psalter:
  "A furore Normanorum,
  Libera nos, O Domine!"

But you hold that quick repentance
  In the Northern mind will be;
This repentance comes no sooner
Than the robber's did at Luna.*
  "A furore Normanorum,
    Libera nos, O Domine!"

He repented him; the Bishop
  Gave him absolution free—
Poured upon him sacred chrism
In the pomp of his baptism
  "A furore Normanorum,
    Libera nos, O Domine!"

He repented; then, he sickened—
  Was he pining for the sea?
In extremis he was shriven,
The Viaticum was given;
  "A furore Normanorum,
    Libera nos, O Domine!"

---

* The incident with which I have illustrated my opinion of the policy of those who would have us wait for a "reaction at the North," may be found in "Milman's Latin Christianity," vol. iii, p. 133.

Then the old cathedral's choir
  Took the plaintive minor key,
With the Host upraised before him,
Down the marble aisle they bore him,
  "A furore Normanorum,
    Libera nos, O Domine!"

And the Bishop, and the Abbot,
  And the monks of high degree,
Chanting praise to the Madonna,
Came to do him Christian honor.
  "A furore Normanorum,
    Libera nos, O Domine!"

Now, the Miserere's cadence
  Takes the voices of the sea;—
As the music-billows quiver
See the dead freebooter shiver!
  "A furore Normanorum,
    Libera nos, O Domine!"

Is it that those intonations
  Thrill him thus from head to knee?
So! his cerements burst asunder!
'Tis a sight of fear and wonder!
  "A furore Normanorum,
    Libera nos, O Domine!"

Fierce he stands before the Bishop—
 Dark as shape of Destinie!
Hark! a shriek ascends, appalling!
Down the prelate goes, dead—falling;
 "A furore Normanorum,
 Libera nos, O Dominie!"

HASTING lives! He was but feigning!
 What! Repentant? Never he!
Down he smites the priests and friars,
And the city lights with fires.
 "A furore Normanorum,
 Libera nos, O Domine!"

Ah! the children and the maidens,
 'Tis in vain they strive to flee!
Where the white-haired priests lie bleeding
Is no place for tearful pleading.
 "A furore Normanorum,
 Libera nos, O Domine?"

Louder swells the frightful tumult;
 Pallid Death holds reverie;
Dies the organ's mighty clamor,
By the Norseman's iron hammer.
 "A furore Normanorum,
 Libera nos, O Domine!"

And they thought that he repented!
  Had they nailed him to a tree,
He had not deserved their pity,
And—they had not lost their city.
  "A furore Normanorum,
    Libera nos, O Domine!"

There's a moral in this story,
  Which is plain as truth can be:
If we trust the North's relenting,
We will shriek, too late, repenting,
  "A furore Normanorum,
    Libera nos, O Domine!"

GOD SAVE THE SOUTH.

BY REUBEN NASON.

God bless our Southern land!
Guard our beloved land!
  God save the South!
Make us victorious,
Happy and glorious;
Spread Thy shield over us;
  God save the South!

God of our sires, arise!
Scatter our enemies,
    Who mock Thy truth;
Confound their politics,
Frustrate their knavish tricks:
In Thee our faith we fix;
    God save the South!

In the fierce battle-hour,
With Thine almighty power,
    Assist our youth;
May they, with victory crowned,
Joining our choral round,
With heart and voice resound,
    "God save the South!"

ON! SOUTHRON, ON!

BY GEN. M. B. LAMAR.

On! Southron, on!
    Your flag's unfurled
'Mid clashing steel, and death-shot hurled,
And war's dark storm-cloud, swiftly whirled,
    Your country calls. On! Southron, on!

Strike! Southron, strike!
The foeman's trail
  Is marked with blood and flame alike;
And woman's shriek, and infant's wail,
Show that he wars upon the frail
  A war of hate. Strike! Southron, strike!

Can manhood fly,
And, recreant, brave
  The silent scorn, the averted eye—
Decked in its chains—a cringing slave?
No! rather seek a soldier's grave,
  And show the tyrant how to die.

Then, Southron, on!
By all that's dear,
  By feeble age, and childhood's dawn,
By mother's love, and maiden's prayer,
The brother's blood, the sister's tear—
  One glance to Heaven, then, Southron, on!

CIVILE BELLUM.

"In this fearful struggle between North and South there are hundreds of cases in which fathers are arrayed against sons, brothers against brothers."—*American paper.*

Rifleman, shoot me a fancy shot,
   Straight at the heart of yon prowling vidette;
Ring me a ball on the glittering spot,
   That shines on his breast like an amulet!"

"Ah! Captain, here goes for a fine-drawn bead;
   There's music around, when my barrel's in tune."
Crack! went the rifle; the messenger sped,
   And dead from his horse fell the ringing dragoon.

"Now, rifleman, steal through the bushes and snatch
   From your victim some trinket to handsel first blood;
A button, a loop, or that luminous patch,
   That gleams in the moon like a diamond stud."

"O Captain! I staggered and sunk in my track,
  When I gazed on the face of the fallen vidette,
For he looked so like you as he lay on his back,
  That my heart rose upon me and masters me yet.

"But I snatched off the trinket—this locket of gold—
  An inch from the center my lead broke its way,
Scarce grazing the picture, so fair to behold,
  Of a beautiful lady in bridal array."

"Ha! rifleman, fling me the locket—'tis she:
  My brother's young bride—and the fallen dragoon
Was her husband—hush! soldier, 't was heaven's decree;
  We must bury him there by the light of the moon!

"But hark! the far bugles their warning unite;
  War is a virtue—weakness a sin;

There's a lurking and loping around us to-
 night;
Load again, rifleman, keep your hand in!"
     FROM THE ONCE UNITED STATES.
London Once a Week.

"FOLLOW, BOYS! FOLLOW!"

BY MILLIE MAYFIELD.

FOLLOW, brave boys, follow!
 'Tis the roll-call of the drum,
And the bright steel's ringing music,
 With its spirit-stirring hum—
'Tis the tramp of armèd columns,
 Brazen fronted, drawing near,
And the rattle of the sabers
 In the scabbards, that ye hear;
  Follow, follow, 'tis the van, boys,
   So bravely leading on;
  Follow, follow, to a man, boys,
   There's glory to be won!

Follow, follow, saith the mother—
 Follow, follow, saith the wife—

Though ye're dear as our hearts' blood,
 More precious, far than life;
But we would not have ye linger
 While the hated foeman stands
Beside our sacred hearth-stones,
 And desecrates our lands!
  We'll forgive the starting tear, boys,
   'Tis the jewel of the heart,
  That ye may not blush to wear, boys,
   When from loved ones thus ye part.

There's not a Southern matron
 But in her bosom wears
The iron Key of Firmness
 That locketh up her fears;
While ye buckle on your armor,
 She will bid ye safe "God-speed,"
And bear her cross all bravely
 For her precious country's need!
  When our women have such souls, boys,
   Ye must never flinch or quail—
  While the storm of battle rolls, boys,
   Ne'er strike the straining sail!

Our lives are dearly purchased,
 When bondage is the price;

And what is home, where freedom
   Withers 'neath the tyrant's vice?
Better the earthy pillow,
   Better the gory bier,
Where the true-hearted ever
   Will drop the burning tear;
     For think, if ye should fall, boys,
       Ye have not lived in vain—
     On the brave soldier's pall, boys,
       None ever put a stain!

Fling out our glorious banner
   Upon the golden air—
Swear by its stars, Dishonor
   Shall leave no footprint there!
That ye'll plant its broad bars firmly,
   As a barrier to the foe,
From the blue Gulf to the Border,
   From the Sea to Mexico!
     The Southern sky's a-flame, boys,
       Where our stately cities burn,
     But, as monuments of fame, boys,
       Their ashes we'll in-urn!

Oh! inch by inch, repel him,
   The foul invading foe!

Let the sharp saber tell him
  How despots are laid low!
And history's burning pencil
  Will, on her golden page,
Your hero name enamel
  An honor to the age!
    One blow, and we are free, boys,
      Strike firmly, and 'tis done!
    On, on, to Tennessee, boys,
      Oh! follow bravely on!

THE SWORD OF ROBERT LEE.

BY FATHER A. J. RYAN.

Forth from its scabbard, pure and bright,
  Flashed the sword of Lee!
Far in the front of the deadly fight,
High o'er the brave in the cause of Right,
Its stainless sheen, like a beacon light,
  Led us to victory.

Out of its scabbard, where, full long,
  It slumbered peacefully,
Roused from its rest by the battle's song,

Shielding the feeble, smiting the strong,
Guarding the right, avenging the wrong,
    Gleamed the sword of Lee.

Forth from its scabbard, high in air,
    Beneath Virginia's sky—
And they who saw it gleaming there,
And knew who bore it, knelt to swear
That where that sword led they would dare
    To follow—and to die!

Out of its scabbard! Never hand
    Waved sword from stain as free,
Nor purer sword led braver band,
Nor braver bled for a brighter land,
Nor brighter land had a cause so grand,
    Nor cause a chief like Lee!

Forth from its scabbard! How we prayed
    That sword might victor be;
And when our triumph was delayed,
And many a heart grew sore afraid,
We still hoped on while gleamed the blade
    Of noble Robert Lee.

Forth from its scabbard all in vain
  Bright flashed the sword of Lee;
'Tis shrouded now in its sheath again,
It sleeps the sleep of our noble slain,
Defeated, yet without a stain,
  Proudly and peacefully.

BOMBARDMENT OF VICKSBURG.

BY PAUL H. HAYNE.

Dedicated with respect and admiration to Major-General Earl Van Dorn.

For sixty days and upwards
  A storm of shell and shot
Rained round as in a flaming shower,
  But still we faltered not!
"If the noble city perish,"
  Our grand young leader said,
"Let the only walls the foe shall scale
  Be ramparts of the dead!"

For sixty days and upwards
  The eye of heaven waxed dim,

And even throughout God's holy morn,
   O'er Christian's prayer and hymn,
Arose a hissing tumult,
   As if the fiends of air
Strove to engulf the voice of faith
   In the shrieks of their despair.

There was wailing in the houses,
   There was trembling on the marts,
While the tempest raged and thundered,
   'Mid the silent thrill of hearts;
But the Lord, our shield, was with us,
   And ere a month had sped,
Our very women walked the streets,
   With scarce one throb of dread.

And the little children gamboled—
   Their faces purely raised,
Just for a wondering moment,
   As the huge bombs whirled and blazed!
Then turning with silvery laughter
   To the sports which children love,
Thrice mailed in the sweet, instinctive thought,
   That the good God watched above.*

---

* It has been stated, by one professing to have witnessed the fact, that, some weeks after the beginning of this terrific

Yet the hailing bolts fell faster
   From scores of flame-clad ships,
And above us denser, darker,
   Grew the conflict's wild eclipse,
Till a solid cloud closed o'er us,
   Like a type of doom and ire,
Whence shot a thousand quivering tongues
   Of forked and vengeful fire.

But the unseen hands of angels
   These death-shafts warned aside,
And the dove of heavenly mercy
   Ruled o'er the battle tide;
In the houses ceased the wailing,
   And through the war-scarred marts
The people strode with the step of hope
   To the music in their hearts.

COLUMBIA, S. C., *August* 6, 1862.

---

bombardment, not only were ladies seen coolly walking the streets, but that in some parts of the town children were observed at play, only interrupting their sports to gaze and listen at the bursting shells.

"THE YANKEE DEVIL."

BY W. P. RIVERS.

The "Nondescript," or "Yankee Devil," for clearing the harbor, was washed ashore on yesterday at Morris Island, and is now in our possession. It is described as an old scow-like vessel, painted red, with a long protruding beak, and jutting iron prongs and claws, intended for the removal of torpedoes. It was attached to the Passaic, and managed by her during the engagement.—*Charleston Courier.*

The enemy are waiting for a new machine ("Devil") to remove the torpedoes in the harbor, and to have everything in readiness before the attack.—*Same paper.*

HURRAH! hurrah! good news and true,
    Our woes will soon be past ;
To Charleston, boys, all praise be due,
    The devil's caught at last.

He's caught, he's dead, and met his fate
    On Morris Island's sands ;
His carcass lies in solemn state,
    The spoil of Rebel hands.

Hurrah! hurrah! let Dixie cheer!
    What may not Charleston do!
The devil's caught at last, we hear;
    A Yankee devil, too!

The blackest, bluest from below,
   The prince of all is he,
Who leads the Yankees where they go,
   On land, or on the sea.

The news is true, all doubt dispel,
   All grief and fears be o'er!
The chiefest from perdition's well
   Lies on a Southern shore.

On South Carolina's beach he lies—
   His majesty ashore!
Ah! well we know that devil dies
   Who enters at that door.

His name and hue, and shape and size,
   Identify the beast;
'Tis he—the father of all lies,
   Of devils not the least.

Scow-like across the deep he came,
   Blood-red his iron sides;
With beak, and claws, and fins of flame
   To plow the vernal tides.

Like serpents which Minerva sent
   To crush the Trojan sire,
So Northern devils come to vent
   On Charleston blood and fire.

But Neptune ne'er decreed the fate
   Of Laocoön's dear sons,
To gratify the Yankees' hate
   On Charleston's dearer ones.

They'll never bear one fatal hour
   The Northern serpent's coil,
Nor feel the Yankee devil's power
   Who come to crush and spoil.

The "Nondescript," name chosen well;
   The "Northern Devil," aye!
A fiend, a ghoul, a spirit fell!
   Who may describe it—say?

Foul, artful, bloody, false, insane,
   This Northern ghote* of sin;
The heathen hells could ne'er contain
   A darker power within.

---

* Ghote—an imaginary evil being among Eastern nations.

But now, hurrah, the devil's dead!
  High, dry upon the shore!
Rebellion still may rear its head,
  The war will soon be o'er.

Hold, not so fast, abate your cheer,
  The battle is not won;
Another devil comes, we hear,
  Before the work is done.

Alas! when will this warfare end?
  Not till all Yankee foes are dead;
For nondescript is each—or fiend—
  His soul with murder red.

CAVE SPRINGS, GA., *April* 11, 1863.

THE BOY-SOLDIER.

BY A LADY OF SAVANNAH.

HE is acting o'er the battle,
  With his cap and feather gay,
Singing out his soldier prattle,
  In a mockish, manly way—

THE BOY-SOLDIER.

With the boldest, bravest footstep,
   Treading firmly up and down,
And his banner waving softly
   O'er his boyish locks of brown.
And I sit beside him sewing,
   With a busy heart and hand,
For the gallant soldiers going
   To the far-off battle-land;
And I gaze upon my jewel,
   In his baby-spirit bold,
My little blue-eyed soldier,
   Just a second summer old.

Still a deep, deep well of feeling,
   In my mother's heart is stirred,
And the tears come softly stealing
   At each imitative word.

There's a struggle in my bosom,
   For I love my darling boy—
He's the gladness of my spirit,
   He's the sunlight of my joy!
Yet I think upon my country,
   And my spirit groweth bold,
Oh! I wish my blue-eyed soldier
   Were but twenty summers old!

I would speed him to the battle,
  I would arm him for the fight,
I would give him to his country,
  For his country's wrong and right!
I would nerve his hand with blessing,
  From the "God of Battles" won;
With *His* helmet and *His* armor,
  I would cover o'er my son.

Oh! I *know* there'd be a struggle,
  For I love my darling boy;
He's the gladness of my spirit,
  He's the sunlight of my joy!
Yet in thinking of my country,
  Oh! my spirit groweth bold;
And I wish my blue-eyed soldier
  Were but twenty summers old.

THE VIRGINIANS OF THE VALLEY.

BY FRANK TICKNOR, M. D.

Sic Jurat.

THE knightliest of the knightly race,
  Who, since the days of old,

Have kept the lamp of chivalry
  Alight in hearts of gold;
The kindliest of the kindly band
  Who rarely hated ease,
Who rode with Smith around the land
  And Raleigh round the seas!

Who climbed the blue Virginia hills,
  Amid embattled foes,
And planted there, in valleys fair,
  The lily and the rose;
Whose fragrance lives in many lands,
  Whose beauty stars the earth,
And lights the hearths of many homes
  With loveliness and worth!

We thought they slept! the sons who kept
  The names of noble sires,
And slumbered while the darkness crept
  Around their vigil fires!
But still the Golden Horseshoe knights,
  Their Old Dominion keep,
Whose foes have found enchanted ground,
  But not a knight asleep.

  TORCH HALL, GA.

C. S. A.

BY FATHER ABRAM J. RYAN.

Do we weep for the heroes who died for us,
Who, living, were true and tried for us,
And, dying, sleep side by side for us;
    The martyr band
    That hallowed our land
With the blood they shed in a tide for us?

Ah! fearless on many a day for us,
They stood in the front of the fray for us,
And held the foeman at bay for us;
    And tears should fall
    Fore'er o'er all
Who fell while wearing the gray for us.

How many a glorious name for us,
How many a story of fame for us
They left: Would it not be a blame for us
    If their memories part
    From our land and heart,
And a wrong to them, and a shame for us?

No, no, no! they were brave for us,
And bright were the lives they gave for us;

The land they struggled to save for us
    Will not forget
    Its warriors yet
Who sleep in so many a grave for us.

On many and many a plain for us
Their blood poured down all in vain for us,
Red, rich, and pure, like a rain for us;
    They bleed—we weep,
    We live—they sleep,
"All lost," the only refrain for us.

But their memories e'er shall remain for us,
And their names, bright names, without stain
    for us;
The glory they won shall not wane for us,
    In legend and lay
    Our heroes in gray
Shall forever live over again for us.

THE SWEET SOUTH.

BY WILLIAM GILMORE SIMMS.

O THE sweet South! the sunny, sunny South!
   Land of true feeling, land forever mine!
I drink the kisses of her rosy mouth,
   And my heart swells as with a draught of wine;
She brings me blessings of maternal love;
   I have her smile which hallows all my toil;
Her voice persuades, her generous smiles approve,
   She sings me from the sky and from the soil!
O, by her lonely pines that wave and sigh!
   O, by her myriad flowers, that bloom and fade,
By all the thousand beauties of her sky,
   And the sweet solace of her forest shade,
      She's mine—she's ever mine—
      Nor will I aught resign
Of what she gives me, mortal or divine;
      Will sooner part
      With life, hope, heart—
Will die—before I fly!

O, love is hers—such love as ever glows
   In souls where leap affection's living tide;

She is all fondness to her friends; to foes
   She glows a thing of passion, strength, and
      pride ;
She feels no tremors when the danger's nigh,
   But the fight over and the victory won,
How, with strange fondness, turns her loving eye
   In tearful welcome on each gallant son!
O! by her virtues of the cherished past—
   By all her hopes of what the future brings—
I glory that my lot with her is cast,
   And my soul flushes and exulting sings;
      She's mine—she's ever mine—
     For her will I resign
All precious things—all placed upon her shrine;
      Will freely part
      With life, hope, heart—
Will die—do aught but fly!

THE SOUTHERN CROSS.*

BY MRS. ELLEN KEY BLUNT.

In the name of God! Amen!
  Stand for our Southern rights!
Arm, ye Southern men,
  The God of Battle fights!
Fling the invaders far,
  Hurl back their work of woe,
The voice is the voice of a brother,
  But the hands are the hands of a foe.
They come with a trampling army,
  Invading our native sod—
Stand, Southrons! fight and conquer!
  In the name of the Mighty God!

They're singing *our* song of triumph †
  Which was made to make us free,
While they're breaking away the heartstrings
  Of our nation's harmony.

---

* These lines were dedicated "to His Excellency President Davis, from his fellow-citizens, Ellen Key Blunt, J. T. Mayson Blunt, of Maryland and Virginia."

† "The Star-Spangled Banner," written by Francis Scott Key, a progenitor of Mrs. Blunt.

Sadly it floateth from us,
   Sighing o'er land and wave,
Till mute on the lips of the poet,
   It sleeps in his Southern grave.
Spirit and song departed!
   Minstrel and minstrelsy!
We mourn thee, heavy-hearted,
   But we will, we shall be free!

They are waving *our* flag above us,
   With a despot's tyrant will;
With our blood they have stained its colors,
   And call it holy still.
With tearful eyes, but steady hand,
   We'll tear its stripes apart,
And fling them like broken fetters,
   That may not bind the heart;
But we'll save our stars of glory,
   In the might of the sacred sign
Of Him who has fixed forever
   Our Southern Cross to shine.

Stand, Southrons! stand and conquer!
   Solemn and strong and sure!
The strife shall not be longer
   Than God shall bid endure.

By the life which only yesterday
   Came with the infant's breath,
By the feet which ere the morn may
   Tread to the soldier's death!
By the blood which cries to Heaven!
   Crimson upon our sod!
Stand, Southrons! stand and conquer!
   In the name of the Mighty God!
     PARIS, 1862.

PATRIOTISM.

THE holy fire that nerved the Greek
   To make his stand at Marathon,
Until the last red foeman's shriek
   Proclaimed that Freedom's fight was won,
Still lives unquenched—unquenchable!
   Through every age its fires will burn—
Lives in the hermit's lonely cell,
   And springs from every storied urn!

The hearthstone embers hold the spark
   Where fell Oppression's foot hath trod;
Through Superstition's shadow dark
   It flashes to the living God!

From Moscow's ashes spring the Russ;
  In Warsaw Poland lives again;
Schamyl, on frosty Caucasus,
  Strikes Liberty's electric chain!

Tell's freedom-beacon lights the Swiss;
  Vainly the invader ever strives;
He finds "Sic Semper Tyrannis"
  In San Jacinto's bowie-knives!
Than these—than all—a holier fire
  Now burns thy soul, Virginia's son!
Strike then for wife, babe, gray-haired sire;
  Strike for the grave of Washington!

The Northern rabble aims for greed;
  The hireling parson goads the train—
In that foul crop from bigot seed,
  Old "Praise God Barebones" howls again!
We welcome them to "Southern lands"—
  We welcome them to "Southern slaves"—
We welcome them "with bloody hands
  To hospitable Southern graves!"

SONG FOR THE MARYLAND LINE.

BY J. D. M'CABE, JR.

By old Potomac's rushing tide
  Our bayonets are gleaming;
And o'er the bounding waters wide
  We gaze while tears are streaming.
The distant hills of Maryland
  Rise sadly up before us,
And tyrant bands have chained our land—
  Our mother, proud, that bore us.

Our proud old mother's queenly head
  Is bowed in subjugation;
With her children's blood her soil is red,
  And fiends in exultation
Taunt her with shame as they bind her chains,
  While her heart is torn with anguish;
Old mother, on famed Manassas's plains
  Our vengeance did not languish!

We thought of your wrongs as on we rushed,
  'Mid shot and shell appalling;
We heard your voice as it upward gushed
  From the Maryland life-blood falling.

No pity we knew! Did they mercy show
    When they bound the mother that bore us?
But we scattered death 'mid the dastard foe,
    Till they, shrieking, fled before us!

We mourn for our brothers brave, that fell
    On that field, so stern and gory;
But their spirits rose with our triumph-yell
    To the heavenly realms of glory.
And their bodies rest on the hard-won field—
    By their love so true and tender;
We'll keep the prize they would not yield,
    We'll die, but we'll not surrender.

And, mother, we wait but the signal-blast,
    To rush to redeem thy glory;
We may fall, but our conquering dust shall rest
    On thy soil, so famed in story.
The tyrant's flag shall no longer shine,
    Thy liberty to smother,
When the word is passed to the Maryland Line,
    To strike for their loved old mother.

CONFEDERATE LAND.

BY H. H. STRAWBRIDGE.

States of the South! Confederate land!
   Our foe has come—the hour is nigh;
His bale-fires rise on every hand—
   Rise as one man, to do or die!
From mountain, vale, and prairie wide,
   From forest vast, and field, and glen,
And crowded city, pour thy tide,
   Oh! fervid South! of patriot men.
       Up! old and young; the weak, be strong!
       Rise for the right—hurl back the wrong,
       And foot to foot, and hand to hand,
       Strike for our own Confederate land!

Make every house, and rock, and tree,
   And hill, your forts; and fen and flood
Yield not! our soil shall rather be
   One waste of flame, one sea of blood!
Fear not their steel, but fear their gold—
   Not Yankee force, but Yankee fraud;
Trust not the race—as false as cold—
   Whose very prayers are lies to God.
       Up! old and young, etc.

Armed, or unarmed, stand fearless forth,
  Sons of the South! stand, wife and maid!
Against the foul insidious North,
  Our *babes* shall wield the battle-blade!
On! though perennial be the strife,
  For honor dear, for hearth-stone fire;
Give blow for blow! take life for life!
  "Strike! till the last armed foe expire!"
    Up! old and young, etc.

THE BANNER SONG.

BY JAMES B. MARSHALL.

Up, up with the banner, the foe is before us,
  His bayonets bristle, his sword is unsheathed,
Charge, charge on his line with harmonious chorus,
  For the prayers go with us that beauty has breathed.

He fights for the power of despot and plunder,
  While we are defending our altars and homes;
He has riven the firmly-knit Union asunder,
  And to bind it with Tyranny's fetters he comes.

Like the prophet Mokanna, whose veil so re-
    splendent,
  His monstrous deformity closely concealed,
Duplicity marks Lincoln's course, and dependent
  On falsehood is every fair promise revealed.

When that veil shall be raised, Freedom's last
    feast be taken,
  A banquet to which all his followers will
    crowd;
Oh, horror of horrors! who can view it un-
    shaken?
  Without sense they will sit all in suppliance
    bowed!
We do not forget that they once were our
    brothers,
  That we sat in our boyhood around the same
    board,
That our heart's best idolatry blest the same
    mothers,
  And to the same fathers libations we poured.

We rallied around the same star-spangled stand-
    ard,
  When called to the field by the tocsin of war:

But they from our side have unfeeling wandered,
    And we strip from our flag every recusant star.
They have forced us to stand by our own Constitution,
    To defend our lov'd homesteads, our altars and fires,
While they tamely submit to a tyrant's pollution,
    Beneath whose foul tread their own freedom expires.

Then up with the banner, its broad stripes wide flowing—
    'Tis the emblem of Liberty—flag of the free;
Let it wave us to triumph, and every heart glowing,
    Nerve each arm's bravest blow for its lov'd Tennessee.

THE SOUTHERN HOMES IN RUINS.

BY R. B. VANCE.

Many a gray-haired sire has died,
   As falls the oak, to rise no more,
Because his son, his prop, his pride,
   Breathed out his last all red with gore.
No more on earth, at morn, at eve,
   Shall age and youth, entwined as one—
Nor father, son, for either grieve—
   Life's work, alas, for both is done!

Many a mother's heart has bled
   While gazing on her darling child,
As in its tiny eyes she read
   The father's image, kind and mild;
For ne'er again his voice will cheer
   The widowed heart, which mourns him dead;
Nor kisses dry the scalding tear,
   Fast falling on the orphan's head!

Many a little form will stray
   Adown the glen and o'er the hill,
And watch with wistful looks the way
   For him whose step is missing still;

And when the twilight steals apace
　　O'er mead, and brook, and lonely home,
And shadows cloud the dear, sweet face—
　　The cry will be, "Oh, papa, come!"

And many a home's in ashes now,
　　Where joy was once a constant guest,
And mournful groups there are, I trow,
　　With neither house nor place of rest;
And blood is on the broken *sill*,*
　　Where happy feet went to and fro,
And everywhere, by field and hill,
　　Are sickening sights and sounds of woe;

There is a God who rules on high,
　　The widow's and the orphan's friend,
Who sees each tear and hears each sigh
　　That these lone hearts to Him may send!
And when in wrath He tears away
　　The reasons vain which men indite,

---

* These lines were suggested by the following, published in "Frank Leslie's Illustrated Newspaper": "We know a great deal about war now; but, dear readers, the Southern women know more. Blood has not dripped on our *door-sills* yet; shells have not burst above our *homesteads*. Let us pray they never may."

The record-book will plainest say
  Who's in the wrong, and who is right.

'TIS MIDNIGHT IN THE SOUTHERN SKY.

BY MRS. M. J. YOUNG.

'Tis midnight in the Southern sky—
  See the starry cross decline!
The watching flowers, all bath'd in tears,
  Creep o'er the mournful sign!

But that decline but serves to mark
  A bright and glorious hour,
Whose gleaming splendors shall then crown
  With stars the simplest flower!

A day that in its turn shall tell
  Of the starry cross uprighted!
Then weep not—ev'ry change is well—
  All wrongs shall be requited!

"STACK ARMS."

BY JOSEPH BLYTHE ALSTON.[*]

"Stack arms!" I've gladly heard the cry,
   When, weary with the dusty tread
Of marching troops, as night grew nigh,
   And sank upon my soldier bed,
And calmly slept; the starry dome
   Of heaven's blue arch my canopy,
And mingled with my dreams of home,
   The thoughts of Peace and Liberty.

"Stack arms!" I've heard it, when the shout,
   Exulting, rang along our line,
Of foes hurled back in bloody rout,
   Captured, dispersed; its tones divine
Then came to mine enraptured ear,
   Guerdon of duty nobly done,
And glistened on my cheek the tear
   Of grateful joy for victory won.

"Stack arms!" In faltering accents, slow
   And sad, it creeps from tongue to tongue,

---

[*] Written in the prison of Fort Delaware, Del., on hearing of General Lee's surrender.

A broken, murmuring wail of woe,
   From manly hearts by anguish wrung.
Like victims of a midnight dream,
   We move, we know not how nor why,
For life and hope but phantoms seem,
   And it would be relief—to die.

THE INVOCATION.

BY B. W. W.

GOD bless the land of flowers,
And turn its winter hours
   To bright summer time!
Be the brave soldier's friend,
And from dangers defend,
When Northern balls descend
   On the Southern line!

Father, we implore Thee,
Let Thy people go free
   From their foes once more!
And they will bend the knee,
And Thine the praise shall be,

On sunny land and sea,
    As in days of yore!

Lord, bid the carnage cease,
Let the banner of peace
    Again be unfurled!
Two nations make from one,
And when the work is done,
Over both reign alone—
    Saviour of the world!

DOFFING THE GRAY.

BY LIEUTENANT FALLIGANT.

OFF with your gray suits, boys,
  Off with your rebel gear!
They smack too much of the cannon's peal,
The lightning flash of your deadly steel,
  The terror of your spear.

Their color is like the smoke
  That curled o'er your battle-line;
They call to mind the yell that woke

When the dastard columns before you broke,
  And their dead were your fatal sign.

Off with the starry wreath,
  Ye who have led our van;
To you 'twas the pledge of glorious death,
When we followed you over the gory heath,
  Where we whipped them man to man.

Down with the cross of stars—
  Too long hath it waved on high;
'Tis covered all over with battle-scars,
But its gleam the Northern banner mars—
  'Tis time to lay it by.

Down with the vows we've made,
  Down with each memory—
Down with the thoughts of our noble dead—
Down, down to the dust, where their forms are laid,
  And down with Liberty.

THE CONFEDERATE FLAG.

BY FATHER A. J. RYAN.

Take that banner down, 'tis weary,
Round its staff 'tis drooping dreary,
　Furl it, hide it, let it rest;
For there's not a man to wave it—
For there's not a soul to lave it
In the blood that heroes gave it.
　Furl it, hide it, let it rest.

Take that banner down, 'tis tattered;
Broken is its staff, and shattered;
And the valiant hearts are scattered
　Over whom it floated high.
Oh! 'tis hard for us to fold it—
Hard to think there's none to hold it—
Hard that those who once unrolled it,
　Now must furl it with a sigh.

Furl that banner, furl it sadly;
Once six millions hailed it gladly,
And three hundred thousand madly,
　Swore it should forever wave—

Swore that foeman's sword should never
Hearts like theirs entwined dissever—
That their flag should float forever
  O'er their freedom or their grave!

Furl it, for the hands that grasped it,
And the hearts that fondly clasped it,
  Cold and dead are lying low;
And that banner—it is trailing,
While around it sounds the wailing
  Of its people in their woe;
For though conquered, they adore it,
Love the cold, dead hands that bore it,
Weep for those who fell before it—
Oh! how wildly they deplore it,
  Now to furl and fold it so!

Furl that banner; true 'tis gory,
But 'tis wreathed around with glory,
And 'twill live in song and story,
  Though its folds are in the dust;
For its fame, on brightest pages—
Sung by poets, penned by sages—
Shall go sounding down to ages—
  Furl its folds though now we must.

Furl that banner—softly, slowly;
Furl it gently, it is holy,
   For it droops above the dead.
Touch it not, unfurl it never,
Let it droop there, furled forever,
   For its people's hopes are fled.

FOLD IT UP CAREFULLY.

GALLANT nation, foiled by numbers,
   Say not that your hopes are fled;
Keep that glorious flag which slumbers,
   One day to avenge your dead.

Keep it till your children take it,
Once again to hail and make it
All their sires have bled and fought for,
All their noble hearts have sought for,
   Bled and fought for all alone.
All alone! aye, shame the story,
   Millions here deplore the stain,
Shame, alas! for England's glory,
   Freedom called, and called in vain.

Furl that banner, sadly, slowly,
Treat it gently, for 'tis holy:
'Till that day—yes, furl it sadly,
Then once more unfurl it gladly—
   Conquered Banner—keep it still!*

WHY CAN NOT WE BE BROTHERS?

BY CLARENCE PRENTICE.

Why can not we be brothers? the battle now is o'er;
We've laid our bruis'd arms on the field, to take them up no more;
We who have fought you hard and long, now overpower'd stand
As poor defenseless prisoners in our own native land.
Chorus—We know that we are Rebels,
   And we don't deny the name,
   We speak of that which we have done
   With grief, but not with shame.

---

* A reply to "The Conquered Banner," by Sir Henry Houghton, Bart., of Great Britain.

But we have rights most sacred, by solemn com-
 pact bound,
Seal'd by the blood that freely gush'd from many
 a ghastly wound;
When Lee gave up his trusty sword, and his
 men laid down their arms,
It was that they should live at home, secure
 from war's dire harms.

And surely, since we've now disarm'd, we are not
 to be dreaded;
Our old chiefs, who on many fields our trusty
 columns headed,
Are fast within an iron grasp, and manacled
 with chains,
Perchance, 'twixt dreary walls to stay as long
 as life remains!

Oh! shame upon the coward band. who in the
 conflict dire,
Went not to battle for their cause, 'mid the
 ranks of steel and fire,
Yet now, since all the fighting's done, are hourly
 heard to cry:
"Down with the traitors! hang them all, each
 Rebel dog shall die!"

We know that we were Rebels, we don't deny the name,
We speak of that which we have done with grief, but not with shame!
And we never will acknowledge that the blood the South has spilt,
Was shed defending what we deem'd a cause of wrong and guilt.

REUNITED.

BY FATHER ABRAM J. RYAN.*

Purer than thy own white snow,
   Nobler than thy mountain's height,
Deeper than the ocean's flow,
   Stronger than thy own proud might;
Oh! Northland, to thy sister land
Was late thy mercy's generous deed and grand.

Nigh twice ten years the sword was sheathed;
   Its mist of green o'er battle plain
For nigh two decades spring had breathed;
   And yet the crimson life-blood stain
From passive swards had never paled,
Nor fields, where all were brave and some had
     failed.

---

* Written after the yellow-fever epidemic of 1878.

Between the Northland, bride of snow,
   And Southland, brightest sun's fair bride,
Swept, deepening ever in its flow,
   The stormy wake, in war's dark tide:
No hand might clasp across the tears,
And blood, and anguish of four deathless years.

When summer, like a rose in bloom,
   Had blossomed from the bud of spring,
Oh! who could deem the dews of doom
   Upon the blushing lips could cling?
And who could believe its fragrant light
Would e'er be freighted with the breath of blight?

Yet o'er the Southland crept the spell,
   That e'en from out its brightness spread;
And prostrate, powerless, she fell,
   Rachel-like, amid her dead.
Her bravest, fairest, purest, best,
The waiting grave would welcome, as its guest.

The Northland, strong in love, and great,
   Forgot the stormy days of strife;
Forgot that souls with dreams of hate,
   Or unforgiveness, e'er were rife.

Forgotten was each thought and hushed,
Save—she was generous and her foe was crushed.

No hand might clasp, from land to land;
   Yea! there was one to bridge the tide;
For at the touch of Mercy's hand
   The North and South stood side by side:
The Bride of Snow, the Bride of Sun,
In Charity's espousals are made one.

"Thou givest back my sons again,"
   The Southland to the Northland cries;
"For all my dead, on battle plain,
   Thou biddest my dying now uprise:
I still my sobs, I cease my tears,
And thou hast recompensed my anguished years.

"Blessings on thine every wave,
   Blessings on thine every shore,
Blessings that from sorrows save,
   Blessings giving more and more,
For all thou gavest thy sister land,
Oh! Northland, in thy generous deed and grand."

INDEX.

A Ballad of the War. George Herbert Sass, 179.
A Cry to Arms. Henry Timrod, 72.
"A. M. W.," 68.
Address of the Women to the Southern Troops. Mrs. Jane T. H. Cross, 160.
Alexandria, The Martyr of, 36.
Alston, Joseph Blythe, of South Carolina, 305.
A New Red, White, and Blue. Jeff Thompson, 153.
Antrobur, John, 196.
A Poem for the Times. John R. Thompson, 5.
A Poem which Needs no Dedication. James Barron Hope, 264.
"A Rebel," 92.
Arise. C. G. Poynas, 20.
Arm for the Southern Land. Mirabeau B. Lamar, 235.
"A Soldier's Wife," 256
"Atlanta Confederacy," 62.

Ballard, Sallie E., of Texas, 44.
Band in the Pines, The. John Esten Cooke, 230.
Banner Song, The. James B. Marshall, 299.
Barrick, J. R., of Kentucky, 192.
Battle-field of Manassas, The. M. F. Bigney, 98.
Battle at Bull Run, The. "Ruth," 137.
Battle-Call. Annie Chambers Ketchum, 131.
Beaufort, F. P., 108.
Beauregard Songster, The, 171.
Bell, Maurice, 190.
Beyond the Potomac. Paul H. Hayne, 204.
Bigney, M. F., 98, 126.
Blue Cockade, The. Mary Walsingham Crean, 83.
Blunt, Mrs. Ellen Key, 292.
Bombardment of Vicksburg. Paul H. Hayne, 278.
Bonnie Blue Flag, The. Harry Macarthy, 135.

Box, Rev. A. M., 78.
Boy-Soldier, The. A Lady of Savannah, 284.
Burgess, G. T., 172.
Burn the Cotton. "Estelle," 211.
"B. W. W.," 306.

Call All! Call All! "Georgia," 31.
Canedo, Mrs. Margarita J., 199.
"Caroline," 23.
Cavaliers of Dixie, The. Benj. F. Porter, 162.
"Charleston Mercury," 23.
Chivalrous C. S. A. "B.," 96.
Civile Bellum. "The Once United States," 271.
"C. L. S.," 175.
Confederate Flag, The. J. R. Barrick, 192.
Confederate Flag, The. Mrs. C. D. Elder, 222.
Confederate Flag, The. Father A. J. Ryan, 309.
Confederate Land. By H. H. Strawbridge, 298.
"Confederate Prisoner," 226.
Confederate Song. Capt. E. Lloyd Wailes, 109.
Cooke, John Esten, 230.
"Cora," 252.
Crean, Mary Walsingham, 83.
Cross, Mrs. J. T. H., 160.
C. S. A. Father Ryan, 288.
Cummins, Alex. H., 248.

Dixie. Albert Pike, 38.

"De G.," 81.
Doffing the Gray. Lieutenant Falligant, 307.
Dying Soldier, The. James A. Mecklin, 239.

Elbert, Evan, 27.
Elder, Mrs. C. D., 222.
Estelle, 211, 260.
Estres, William C., 243.
Ethnogenesis. Henry Timrod, 9.

Falligant, Lieutenant, of Savannah, Georgia, 307.
Farewell to Brother Jonathan. "Caroline," 23.
Flash, Henry L., of Texas, 85, 246.
"Follow, Boys, Follow!" Millie Mayfield, 273.
Fold it up Carefully. Sir Henry Houghton, 311.
Freer, M. C., 111.
French, L. Virginia, 129.
From the South to the North. C. L. S., 175.

"Georgia," 31.
Girls of the Monumental City. "Confederate Prisoner," 226.
God Save the South. Reuben Nason, 268.
Gone to the Battle-field. John Antrobur, 196.
Gray, Nanny, 30.
Guerillas, The. S. Teackle Wallis, 166.

INDEX. 321

Harp of the South. "Cora," 252.
Harp of the South, Awake. J. M. Kilgour, 17.
Hayne, Paul H., 204, 278.
Heart of Louisiana, The. Harriet Stanton, 63.
Heart Victories. "A Soldier's Wife," 256.
"H. M. L.," 128.
Holcombe, Wm. H., of Louisiana, 77.
Holtz, Robert E., 149.
Hood, Thomas B., 139.
Hope, James Barron, 264.
Houghton, Sir Henry, Bart., 312.

Invocation, The. B. W. W., 306.

Jackson. Henry L. Flash, 246.
Jackson, Gen. H. R., of Louisiana, 114.
Jacobus, Mrs. J. J., 33.
"J. H. H.," 66.
Johnson, Bradley T., 19.
Justice is our Panoply. De G., 81.

Kentucky. "Estelle," 260.
Ketchum, Anna Chambers, 131.
Keyes, Julia L., of Ala., 121.
Kilgour, J. M., 17.
Killum, John, 233.

Lamar, Gen. M. B., 235, 269.
Land of King Cotton. Jo. Augustine Signiago, 164.

Land of the South. A. F. Leonard, 185.
Legion of Honor, The. H. L. Flash, 85.
Leonard, A. F., 185.
Lomas, Henry, 253.
Lorrimer, Laura, 142.

Macarthy, Harry, 135.
Manassas. "A Rebel," 92.
Marseilles Hymn, The. B. F. Porter, of Alabama, 216.
Marshall, James B., 299.
Martin, Rev. J. H., 45.
Martyr of Alexandria, The. James W. Simmons, 36.
Mayfield, Millie, 90, 249, 273.
Maryland. James R. Randall, 69.
McCabe, J. D., Jr., 296.
McLemore, John C., of South Carolina, 87.
Mecklin, James A., 239.
Meek, A. B., of Mobile, Alabama, 52.
Melt the Bells. F. Y. Rockett. 47.
Miles, George H., of Balt., 123.
Monody on the Death of Gen. Stonewall Jackson. "The Exile," 220.
Moore, Emily J., 210.
"M. S.," 241.
Murden, E. O., 54.
My Wife and Child. Gen. H. R. Jackson, of Louisiana, 114.

Nason, Reuben, 268.

New Orleans " True Delta," 43.
" Nil Desperandum." Ada Rose, 158.
No Surrender. "N. P. W.," 234.
No Union Men. Millie Mayfield, 249.
" N. P. W.," 146, 234.

O Johnny Bull, my Jo John, 154.
Old Betsy. John Killum, 233.
Old Rifleman, The. Frank Ticknor, M. D., 119.
Only One Killed. Julia L. Keyes, 121.
On! Southron, on! M. B. Lamar, 269.
Ordered Away, The. Mrs. J. J. Jacobus, 33.
Our Boys are Gone. Col. Hamilton Washington, 141.
Overall, John W., of La., 41, 145, 259.

Patriotism, 294.
" P. E. C.," 116.
Pensacola, To my Son. M. S., 241.
Pierpont, James, 29.
Pike, Albert, of Arkansas, 38.
Porter, Benjamin F., of Alabama, 162, 216, 228.
Poynas, C. G., of South Carolina, 20.
Prentice, Clarence, 312.
Printers of Virginia to Old Abe, The. Harry C. Treakle, 214.
Prize Song, The, 201.

Randall, James R., of Maryland, 69, 188.
Rebels! 'tis a Holy Name! "Atlanta Confederacy," 61.
Re-enlistment. Mrs. Margarita J. Canedo, 199.
Requier, A. J., of Alabama, 143.
Reunited. Father Ryan, 315.
" Richmond Examiner," 52.
Richmond on the James. G. T. Burgess, 172.
Right Above the Wrong, The. John W. Overall, 41.
Rivers, Pearl, 208.
Rivers, W. P., 281.
Rockett, F. Y., 47.
Rose, Ada, 158.
" Ruth," 137.
Ryan, Father A. J., 276, 288, 309, 315.

Sass, George Herbert, of South Carolina, 179.
Savannah, A Lady of, 284.
Seventy-Six and Sixty-One. John W. Overall, 259.
Signiago, Jo. Augustine, 164.
Simmons, Jas. W., of Texas, 36.
Simms, Wm. Gilmore, 290.
Soldier Boy, The. H. M. L., 128.
Soldier's Heart, The. F. P. Beaufort, 108.
Song for the Maryland Line. J. D. McCabe, Jr., 296.
Song of the Glorious Southland. Mrs. Mary Ware, 231.

Song of the Privateer. Alex. H. Cummins, 248.
Sons of Freedom. Nanny Gray, 30.
South in Arms, The. Rev. J. H. Martin, 45.
South is Up, The. P. E. C., 116.
Southern Cross, The. St. George Tucker, 14.
Southern Cross, The. Ellen Key Blunt, 292.
Southern Gathering Song. L. Virginia French, 129.
Southern Homes in Ruins, The. R. B. Vance, 302.
Southern Marseillaise. "Beauregard Songster," 170.
Southern Pleiades, The. Laura Lorrimer, 142.
Southern Sentiment. Rev. A. M. Box, 78.
Southern Song. M. C. Freer, 111.
Southern Song of Freedom. J. H. H., 65.
Southern War Song. N. P. W., 146.
Southland. "The Prize Song," 201.
Southern Mother's Charge, The. Thomas B. Hood, 139.
"Southrons." Catharine M. Warfield, 156.
Southron's War Song, The. J. A. Wagener, 80.
"Stack Arms!" J. Blythe Alston, of South Carolina, 305.

Stanton, Harriet, 63.
Stars and Bars, The. A. J. Requier, 143.
Stonewall Jackson's Way, 194.
Strawbridge, H. H., 298.
Sweet South, The. Wm. Gilmore Simms, 290.
Sumter, A Ballad of 1861. E. O. Murden, 54.

Tell the Boys the War is Ended. Emily J. Moore, 210.
"The Exile," 220.
The March. John W. Overall, 145.
The Men. Maurice Bell, 190.
There's Life in the Old Land Yet. J. R. Randall, 183.
There's Nothing going Wrong. A. M. W., 67.
"The South." Charlie Wildwood, 223.
"The Star of the West." "Charleston Mercury," 22.
The Sword of Robert Lee. Father Ryan, 276.
Thinking of the Soldiers, 237.
Thompson, Jeff., 153.
Thompson, John R., of Virginia, 5.
Ticknor, Frank, M. D., of Georgia, 119, 286.
Timrod, Henry, of South Carolina, 9, 72.
'Tis Midnight in the Southern Sky. Mrs. M. J. Young, 304.

To My Soldier Brother. Sallie E. Ballard, 44.
To the Tories of Virginia. "Richmond Examiner," 49.
Treakle, Harry C., 214.
True to the Gray. Pearl Rivers, 208.
Tucker, St. George, of Virginia, 14.
Turtle, The, 245.

Uniform of Gray, The. Evan Elbert, 27.
United States, The Once, 273.
Up! Up! let the Stars of our Banner. M. F. Bigney, 126.

Vance, R. B., of North Carolina, 302.
Virginia: Late but Sure! William H. Holcombe, 77.
Virginians of the Valley. Frank Ticknor, M. D., 286.
Volunteers to the Melish. W. C. Estres, 243.

Wagener, J. A., of South Carolina, 80.
Wailes, Capt. E. Lloyd, 109.
Wallis, S. Teackle, of Maryland, 166.
War Christian's Thanksgiving, The. George H. Miles, of Maryland, 123.
Ware, Mrs. Mary, 231.
Warfield, Catharine M., of Mississippi, 156.
War Song. A. B. Meek, of Mobile, 52.
War Song. By a Lady, 75.
War Song. J. H. Woodcock, 151.
War Song of the Partisan Rangers. B. F. Porter, 228.
Washington, Col. Hamilton, of Texas, 141.
"We Come! We Come!" Millie Mayfield, 90.
We Conquer or Die. James Pierpont, 29.
We'll be Free in Maryland. Robert E. Holtz, 149.
What the Spirits of the Fathers say. Henry Lomas, 253.
"What the Village Bell said." John McLemore, 87.
Whoop! the Doodles, 31.
Why can not We be Brothers? Clarence Prentice, 312.
Wildwood, Charlie, 223.
Woodcock, J. H., 151.

Yankee Devil, The. W. P. Rivers, 281.
Young, Mrs. M. J., 304.

THE END

www.ingramcontent.com/pod-product-compliance
Lightning Source LLC
Chambersburg PA
CBHW030742230426
43667CB00007B/809